THE HBCU EXPERIENCE

The Virginia State University Edition

Visionary Author Ashley Little
Lead Author Jahliel Thurman
President Letter: Makola M. Abdullah, Ph.D
Foreword Author: Franklin H. Johnson, Jr.

For permission requests, write to the publisher, addressed|

"Attention Permissions Coordinator," at
thehbcuexperiencemovement@gmail.com

Book Cover Design: The Harbor Institute

Published By: The HBCU Experience Movement, LLC

The HBCU Experience Movement, LLC
thehbcuexperiencemovement@gmail.com

Ordering Information:

Quantity Sales: Special discounts are available on quantity purchases by corporations, associations, and nonprofits. For details, contact the publisher at the address above.

ISBN: 978-1-7349311-1-2

Dear Trojan Nation,

It is an honor to serve as the 14th President of Virginia State University. From the moment I assumed this position, I have consistently been impressed by the vigor, dedication, and support of our alumni all around the globe. You display an unmatched sense of pride in your alma mater. You show evidence that you truly appreciate the far-reaching value of your VSU education.

Our HBCUs remain relevant and continue to have an immense global impact. We have been developing pioneers for more than a century. With your support, we will continue to provide a transformative educational experience for those who matriculate here, High Above the Appomattox.

We are confident that your voices, sentiments, and stories of success will be felt in a resounding way within the pages of this edition of *The HBCU Experience Movement*. As you share your stories within these pages, it is a testament that the value of the HBCU and VSU is priceless.

It is essential that you continue to tell your stories and share how your lives have been impacted by the transformative experiences at your VSU. We are excited that *The HBCU Experience Movement* has given us an additional platform to tell our story.

Hail State, Hail State, Hail, Hail, Hail.

All my best to each of you,

Makola M. Abdullah, Ph.D.
President, Virginia State University

MAKOLA M. ABDULLAH, PH.D.

About Makola M. Abdullah, Ph.D.

On February 1, 2016, Makola M. Abdullah, Ph.D. became the 14th President of Virginia State University (VSU). In his remarks during his introduction to the Trojan family, President Abdullah outlined his four core beliefs: *I believe in God. I believe in family. I believe in the transformative nature of education. I believe in Virginia State University.*

President Abdullah also emphasized several focus areas to sustain VSU as an 1890 Land-Grant University. The areas of focus include providing a transformative experience for students, strategically investing in academic programs, partnering with others as a university to tell the VSU story, embracing the University's Land Grant Mission and embracing VSU's role as *Virginia's Opportunity University.*

Under President Abdullah's leadership, the University has experienced some significant achievements.

Recognized as one of the nation's top 20 "Best Colleges for African Americans" by ESSENCE magazine.

Established partnerships with local public school systems wherein VSU students tutor students in mathematics and reading,

Opened the Academic Center of Excellence as a one-stop hub for first-year students to receive career and academic advising and tutorial services.

In July 2017, the Commonwealth of Virginia Governor Terry McAuliffe presented the inaugural Outstanding State Stewardship Award to VSU for the preservation of Summerseat, an historic house built around 1860 near VSU.

Established the University's Advisory Board for Lesbian Gay Bisexual Transgender Queer/Questioning Intersex Ally+ (LGBTQIA+) Inclusion to investigate ways for the institution to be a more affirming learning environment for all students, faculty and staff within the LGBTQIA+ community.

In June of 2018, the University was named the HBCU of the Year and awarded Best Board of Trustees of the Year and Female Student of the Year by HBCU Digest, an online blog. Additionally, in 2017, President Abdullah was named the HBCU Male President of the Year.

Ranked as the No. 19 historically black college or university (HBCUs) on the 2019 U.S. News & World Report's Best Colleges rankings. This is up 12 spots from the 2018 rankings where the University was ranked No. 31. Also, the University was ranked as the No. 8 public HBCU.

President Abdullah is an academic administrator committed to excellence. He is also an internationally-renowned educator recognized for outstanding research. Prior to his appointment as president of Virginia State University, Dr. Abdullah served as provost and senior vice president at Bethune-Cookman University in Daytona Beach, Fla. (2013-2016), provost and vice president for academic affairs at Florida Memorial University in Miami Gardens, Fla. (2011-2013), and dean and director of 1890 land grant programs at Florida Agricultural and Mechanical University in Tallahassee, Fla (2008-2011).

Dr. Abdullah is a Chicago native. He earned his undergraduate degree from Howard University in civil engineering and his doctorate and master's degrees in civil engineering from Northwestern University. He is the youngest African American to receive a Ph.D. in engineering.

Dr. Abdullah is a very active member with various organizations. In August of 2018, Dr. Abdullah was elected a member of the Board of Trustees for the Virginia Historical Society, which owns and operates the

Virginia Museum of History & Culture. He also serves as a member of the executive committee for the Association of Public and Land-grant Universities, as a Board of Trustee member for the Southern Association of Colleges and Schools Commission on Colleges and the 5000 Role Models of Excellence. He is the chair for the Central Intercollegiate Athletic Association Board of Directors. In 2017, he was inducted into the Honda Campus All-Star Challenge Alumni Hall of Fame. He is a member of Alpha Phi Alpha Fraternity, Incorporated.

He and his wife, Ahkinyala Cobb-Abdullah, Ph.D., are the proud parents of a son, Mikaili, and a daughter, Sefiyetu, who both are college graduates.

A Message from the Founders
Ashley Little, Fred Whit & Uche Byrd

Historically Black Colleges & Universities (HBCUs) were established to serve the educational needs of black Americans. During the time of their establishment, and many years afterward, blacks were generally denied admission to traditionally white institutions. Prior to The Civil War, there was no structured higher education system for black students. Public policy, and certain statutory provisions, prohibited the education of blacks in various parts of the nation. Today, HBCUs represent a vital component of American higher education.

The HBCU Experience Movement, LLC is a collection of stories from prominent alumni throughout the world, who share how their HBCU experience molded them into the people they are today. We are also investing financially into HBCUs throughout the country. Our goal is to create a global movement of prominent HBCU alumni throughout the nation to continue to share their stories each year, allowing us to give back to prestigious HBCUs annually.

We are proud to present to you *The HBCU Experience: The Virginia State University Edition*. We would like to acknowledge and give a special thanks to our amazing lead author/headliner/partner, Jahliel Thurman, for your dedication and commitment. We appreciate you and thank you for your hard work and dedication on behalf of this project. We would also like to give a special thanks to President Makola M. Abdullah Ph.D, foreword author, contributing authors and partners of Virginia State University for believing in this movement and investing your time, and monetary donations, to give back to your school. We appreciate all of the Virginia State University alumni who shared your HBCU experience in this publication.

ASHLEY LITTLE

About Ashley Little

Ashley Little is The CEO/Founder of Ashley Little Enterprises, LLC which encompasses her Media, Consulting Work, Writing, Ghost Writing, Book Publishing, Book Coaching, Project Management, Public Relations & Marketing, and Empowerment Speaking. In addition, she is an Award-Winning Serial Entrepreneur, TV/Radio Host, Speaker, Host, Philanthropist, Business Coach, Investor and 7X Best Selling Author.

She is a proud member of Delta Sigma Theta Sorority Incorporated, and a member of Alpha Phi Omega. She is very involved in her community, organizations and non-profits. Currently, she is the Co-Founder of Sweetheart Scholars Non-profit Organization 501 (C-3) along with three other powerful women. This scholarship is given out annually to African American Females from her hometown of Wadesboro, North Carolina who are attending college to help with their expenses. Ms. Little believes it takes a village to raise a child and to never forget where you come from. Ms. Little is a strong believer in giving back to her community. She believes our young ladies need vision, direction, and strong mentorship. She is the Head of the Scholarship Committee for Swing Into Their Dreams Foundation the mission of Swing Into Their Dream Foundation is E.P.I.C. Empowerment and Philanthropy In The Community. Ms. Little is also the Editor and Chief of Creating Your Seat At The Table Magazine.

She is the Founder and Owner of T.A.L.K Radio & TV Network, LLC. Airs in over 167 countries, streamed LIVE on Facebook, YouTube, Twitter and Periscope. Broadcasting and Media Production Company. This live entertainment platform is for new or existing radio shows, television shows, or other electronic media outlets, to air content from a centralized source. All news, information or music shared on this platform are solely the responsibility of the station/radio owner. She is also the Owner and Creator of Creative Broadcasting Radio Station the station of "unlimited possibilities" and Podcast, Radio/TV Host. She is also one of the hosts of the new TV Show Daytime Drama National Syndicated Television Show which will be aired on Comcast Channel 19 and ATT Channel 99 in 19 Middle Tennessee Counties. It will also air on The United Broadcasting

Network, The Damascus Roads Broadcasting Network, and Roku. She is CEO/Co-Founder of The HBCU Experience Movement LLC and CEO/Founder of Little Publishing LLC.

Ms. Little is a 5X Best Selling Author of "Dear Fear, Volume 2 18 Powerful Lessons Of Living Your Best Life Outside Of Fear", "The Gyrlfriend Code Volume 1", "I Survived", "Girl Get Up, and Win", "Glambitious Guide to Being An Entrepreneur", The Making Of A Successful Business Woman, and "Hello Queen". She is a Co-Host for The Tamie Collins Markee Radio Show, Award-Winning Entrepreneur, Reflection Contributor for the book "NC Girls Living In A Maryland World, Sales/Marketing/Contributing Writer/Event Correspondent for SwagHer Magazine, Contributing Writer for MizCEO Magazine, Contributing Editor for SheIs Magazine, ContributingWriter/National Sales Executive for Courageous Woman Magazine, Contributing Writer for Upwords International Magazine (India), Contributing Writer/Global Partner for Powerhouse Global International Magazine(London), Host of "Creating Your Seat At The Table", Host of "Authors On The Rise", Co-Host Glambitious Podcast, Partner/Visionary Author of The Gyrlfriend Code The Sorority Edition along with The Gyrlfriend Collective, LLC and Lead Author of The HBCU Experience The North Carolina A&T State University Edition. She has been on many different Podcasts, TV Shows, Magazines, and Radio Shows. Lastly, she has received awards such as "Author Of The Month", The Executive Citation of Anne Arundel County, Maryland Award which was awarded by the County Executive Steuart L. Pittman, Top 28 Influential Business Pioneers for K.I.S.H Magazine Spring 2019 Edition. She has been featured in SwagHer Magazine, Power20Magazine Glambitious, Sheen Magazine, All About Inspire Magazine, Formidable Magazine, BRAG Magazine, Sheen Magazine, Front Cover of MizCEO Magazine November 2019, Front Cover for UpWords Magazine October 2019 Edition, Courageous Woman Magazine, Courageous Woman Special Speakers Edition November 2019, Influence Magazine, Featured/Interviewed On a National Syndicated Television Show HBCU 101 on Aspire TV, Dynasty of Dreamers K.I.S.H Magazine Spring 2019 Edition, Dynasty of Dreamers K.I.S.H Magazine September 2019 Edition, Front Cover of Courageous Magazine December 2019, Front

Cover of Doz International Magazine January 2020, Top 28 Influential Business Pioneers for K.I.S.H Magazine, Power20 Magazine Glambitious January 2020, Power20 Magazine Glambitious February 2020, Featured in Powerhouse Global International London Magazine March 2020 edition, Featured in Sheen Magazine February 2020 as one of "The Top 20 Women To Be On The Lookout For In 2020, Awarded National Women's Empowerment Ministry "Young, Gifted, & Black Award" February 2020 which honors and celebrate women in business such as Senior Level Executives, Entrepreneurs and CEO's below age 40 for their creativity and business development. Featured in National Women Empowerment Magazine 2020 as well to name a few.

Ms. Little received her undergraduate degree in English from North Carolina A&T State University. Next, she received her Master's Degree in Industrial Organizational Psychology. Ms. Little is a mover and shaker and she continuously pushes herself to be better than she was yesterday. She gives GOD all the credit for everything that has happened in her life. She has strong faith and determination to be great. She believes her only competition is herself. Her favorite scripture is Philippians 4:13 "I can do all things through Christ who strengthens me".

UCHE BYRD

About Uche Byrd

Uche Byrd was born and raised on the Southside of Chicago. As a graduate from The North Carolina Agricultural and Technical State University, Uche not only obtained his Bachelor's degree in Applied Mathematics, but he also went on to earn a Master's degree in Industrial Engineering. During his tenure at the HBCU, Uche was fortunate enough to pledge the Mu Psi Chapter of Omega Psi Phi Fraternity, Inc., as well as to hold the position of Mr. Aggie. Uche also served as the Region 2 Pre-College Initiative Chair for the National Society of Black Engineers and Vice President of the Midwest Aggie Club. As a Resident Assistant at The Aggie Suites, Uche was a mentor and motivation to many. Today, Uche resides in northeast Washington, D.C. with his wife and son, and serves as the Metro Area Youth Federation Leader for the Allegheny East Conference of the Seventh-Day Adventist Church, where he works with the youth programing for 30+ churches in the D.C., Maryland and Virginia areas.

FRED WHITAKER

About Fred Whitaker

When passion, performance and perseverance come together, a force to be reckoned with is created. Frederick Whitaker, known industry-wide as Fred Whit, has become a well-known name due to his business strategies and negotiative saavy, behind the scenes of the entertainment industry. He is a believer in the mantra hard work pays off, and has lived this mantra everyday of his professional life.

These days, stars such as actor and media personalities Terrence J and La La Anthony, filmmaker Will Packer, and a host of others, call on him when they need unique jobs done in a professional and dignified manner. He rises to any occasion and consistently exceeds expectations.

Growing up between the make or break city of New York and resolute small towns of rural North Carolina, Fred developed his acumen as a polished businessman. New York introduced Fred to the meaning of "hustle" and "ambition" with North Carolina yielding a certain Southern compassion and charm. Now the man the industry sees has the experience and ability to single-handedly take numerous careers to the next level.

As manager of Terrence J (*E! News, Think Like A Man1 & 2*) he secures major roles and television deals and brand integration for the rising star. Fred was instrumental in Terrence landing exclusive endorsements with Crown Royal and Jeep. In addition, Fred successfully planned the rollout for La La Anthony's *New York Times*best seller book, *The Love Playbook: Rules for Love, Sex, and Happiness*. Furthermore, Fred consults for radio host Angela Yee NYC's Power 105 morning show) with more deals in the works. Wearing many hats, he never loses sight of his main goal – to provide incomparable service for each of his clients. Fred proves, as his company motto states, it is the little things you do in life that make all the difference.

Fred has always had a knack for making something out of nothing. While in college at NC A&T State University, he coordinated various large campus events. After graduating with a degree in communications, Fred took steps on a path he didn't imagine himself traveling. "I had no experience in management, so everything I have accomplished over the last fifteen years, I learned on the job," he states. One many occasions he's played the role of assistant, manager, accountant, provided service to whatever was needed for completion. As is this isn't enough, Fred has also negotiated several deals with McDonald's, Sean John, and Samsung, as he goes on to gain favor across multiple branding platforms.

A devout humanitarian, he makes time to organize charity events, toy drives, raising funds and giving away almost $10,000 worth of clothes to the Salvation Army, annually. Fred finds it difficult to build his empire without breathing life into the progress of others.

Success is measured by loving what you do, and making things happen while doing it. As doors continue to open, Fred will never forget those moments where his destiny was uncertain, but he believed his dreams of success would certainly come true. Those dreams have not only come into fruition, they are growing far beyond his imagination. An admirable being and determined man, Fred Whitaker has become a staple in the industry, all while shaping the lives of not only those who achieve fame, but everyday people as well.

Table of Contents Page

FRANKLIN H. JOHNSON, JR.

Foreword

Delegate Alfred W. Harris, the Virginia legislator who introduced the bill creating what would become Virginia State University (VSU) in 1882, dreamt of a place "where all may go and drink from the fountain of knowledge." Over 138 years later that fountain continues to flow and the dream continues to be realized. VSU This dream, however, was note unique to delegate Harris. Historically Black Colleges and Universities (HBCUs) have flourished in the United States since the late 1830s when Quakers founded the African Institute which would eventually become Cheney University of Pennsylvania. For years, HBCUs were the only institutions that Blacks and African Americans could call home for the pursuit of Higher Education.

VSU is the first state supported HBCU in the country and one of two land-grant universities in the commonwealth of Virginia. This cradle of creativity and bastion of brotherhood provides opportunities for growth in areas from agriculture to engineering and education to military sciences. Being on "the hill", as it is referred to by alumni, is an unforgettable experience. HBCU alumni are resilient, resourceful, and remarkable. We lead in every sector of the economy. The University has produced eight United States Army Generals including four-star star General Dennis L. Via. VSU counts amongst its alumni Reginald F. Lewis, the first African American to build a billion dollar company; Miss USA 2016, Deshauna Barber, the first member of the military to win the title; Gladys Mae West a mathematician who greatly contributed to the development of GPS; and Rodney Alexander Robinson 2018 Virginia Teacher of the Year and 2019 National Teacher of the Year.

As this text reveals, the HBCU experience is varied and nuanced. We are not a monolithic people and many of us will not trade our experience for anything. The Trojan Explosion marching band has the distinction of being the first HBCU Marching band to perform inside of the White House while the VSU Gospel Chorale has performed for an audience that included Pope

Francis. As artists and scholars our students and alumni continue to be loyal sons and daughters true to orange and blue.

Currently under the leadership of its 14th President Dr. Makola M. Abdullah, VSU continues to grow, thrive, and serve as Virginia's opportunity University. The Land of Troy is proudly committed to Embracing our Opportunity for Excellence through providing a transformative experience for our students; strategically investing in our academic programs; embracing our position as a top Land Grant University; embracing our role as Virginia's Opportunity University and partnering together as a University to tell our story.

As you read about what makes Virginia State University home, understand that this is only a glimpse into the multifaceted HBCU experience.

Far above the Appomattox,
On its lofty hill,
Stands the school we love so dearly,
And we always will;
Though the years may come between us,
Still whatever our fate,
We will keep thy song before us.
Hail Virginia State.

Franklin H. Johnson, Jr., MBA '04

Virginia State University Alumni Association

National President

JAHLIEL THURMAN

Introduction

What makes Historically Black Colleges and Universities (HBCUs) so unique is the sense of true pride and love one experiences for the African-American community. The support and empowerment one may receive from the HBCU community while seeking to obtain goals and accomplishments is unmatched. In the HBCU community, it does not matter what college you've attended. Once you have become a part of that special bond and community, everyone is looking to lift as they climb. Not only am I grateful to be an HBCU alum, but I am extremely grateful to be a Virginia State University alum. Virginia State University helped develop me into the man I am today in many ways—from learning how to navigate through life many miles away from Chicago, to learning the true art of building relationships.

Virginia State University installed one of the most unique characteristics in me, which is the ability to *adapt*. To be adaptable in society is one of the true keys to success. At the age of 18, being 825 miles away from home can be intimidating. It's out of your comfort zone. However, on my journey, it has been the one thing I have appreciated the most. Studying at Virginia State University taught me that I can go anywhere in the world and be successful.

My goal is to create a source that not only links alums and their stories, but a source that becomes an extension to provide insight to those up and coming about the experience at the illustrious Virginia State University. The authors' wishes are to inspire, motivate and encourage those through their stories and experiences of how Virginia State University transformed them into who they are today. It is extremely essential that HBCU grads give back—not in just monetary ways, but in service because their experiences are priceless. Those experiences should be shared.

The HBCU Experience: Virginia State University Edition is compiled of documented stories from Trojan pioneers throughout the nation. This book highlights Trojans from various eras and all walks of life. We hope every reader enjoys the stories and feels why VSU has a special place in our hearts. Hail State! Hail State! Hail! Hail! Hail!

Lead Author Jahliel Thurman

All The Right Moves
Jahliel Thurman

"Everyone pays for college, son; it is extremely rare that people go to college for free."

These were the words that my mother told me back in fall 2009 when I was applying for college. Now, don't get me wrong—my mother is amazing and supportive. She was just stating her opinion especially because she had never been to college, and this whole process was new to everyone. I then replied, "I'm not paying for college." When I made this statement, I was just being a typical, combative teenager who felt like they knew more than their parents. I was not sure how I was going to attend college for free; however, I love a challenge and proving people wrong.

Interesting enough, my parents had two different ideologies for me going to college. My mom wanted me to stay in state. My dad, however, wanted me to attend an HBCU.

"Go to an HBCU and get the culture," my dad said. "Freshman and sophomore year, enjoy college, maybe pledge a fraternity junior year. Senior year, figure out your next steps and graduate at least magna cum laude."

I chose to listen to my dad.

November 2019, I attended the Siemens Scholarship Reception, a reception for Historically Black Colleges and Universities only. Before the reception, we had an opportunity to check off five schools that we were interested in attending so that they could possibly offer us scholarships. I cannot remember the five schools I chose; however, Virginia State University was one of them. VSU was an option because I had a few high school friends that were currently freshmen; however, I knew absolutely nothing about the university.

As the reception continued, many students' names were called, and I thought I kept getting passed up on. Then VSU was up. They called my name and offered me a lot of money. I remember calling my mom all excited, letting her know what just happened and that "I'm not paying for school." I was going to whatever school offered the most money out of those that I applied to. At that point, I knew I was going to Virginia State University. I called my friends who were freshmen at VSU, and I asked them, "Do you all like it at VSU? Are the Ques on the yard?" They simply responded, "Yes and yes," and that was all I needed to hear.

During my freshman year, I stayed in Langston Hall, which was an honors residence hall. My roommate, Alex Newsom, was from Chicago as well. It was nice to have someone from home as a roommate because we both understood the withdrawals from being so far away from family and friends. A group of us who were from Chicago would eat lunch and dinner together, we hung out together and went to parties together. It was my first family away from home.

Though it sounds like we were all making a way and seemed to be happy, I hated my first semester of college. I hated it because it was a real adjustment in various ways. From living in a fast-paced city to slow Petersburg, not being able to drive freshman year to dealing with being away from my girlfriend at the time, overall, the transition was tough. I even asked my mom to transfer. She said, "Finish the year first, and if you still want to transfer, then you can." I agreed.

The thing about life is that we have phases in which we figure out how to adjust and adapt in our new environments. We are constantly going from being a big fish in a little pond to a little fish in a big pond. With this understanding, I decided I would do more my second semester to get out of my room and meet more people.

One thing that is cool about college is that you can join a club or organization that is not a Greek letter organization. I joined an organization called The Student Liaison Outreach Team (S.L.O.T.) which is a community service-based organization that prides themselves on doing community service and helping out the youth. SLOT instantly became family for me, and this organization allowed me to begin growing into the fish I would later become. Later that semester, I was elected vice president of Administration and Finance of the Student Government Association (SGA). I ended my freshmen year on a *bang*!

Sophomore year, I began to see how fun college could really be. Not just on a party side, but overall. Not only did I move off campus and had my own car, I was doing community service and was enjoying beginning my core classes within my major which was mass communications. Now, the icing on the cake was being in SGA.

I did not realize it at the time, but being in SGA is a big deal at an HBCU. It's a big deal because you are now in an elite group of people. You are now in rooms that students are not in. You travel, you can make change, your network grows, and its beautiful. I was not just a member of SGA though, but I was a VP in which I could really make changes on campus, and I did. For example, one accomplishment I've made was enhancing the dining experience. We had another dining hall built in. This allowed them to alternate days in which the cafes would be open, instead of having both open. This was an issue for students, especially because they were on opposite sides of campus. Long story short, I got them to open both dining halls up every day, and on weekends, they would alternate.

I also created a spice bar. The spice bar is essential because of food allergies. They could not add any unique flavoring to the food, so I wanted students to have the ability to make their food as tasteful as they would like. I had been involved with student government since I was in the sixth grade, but college was the first time it actually meant something to me.

Junior year, I followed the blueprint my father wrote out for me. I joined the greatest fraternity of all time, The Omega Psi Phi Fraternity, Incorporated. Joining this fraternity was one of the best decisions I could have ever made. My probate day is one of the top three best days of my life. The bonds that I've built have changed my life in ways I would never have thought. Being Greek in undergrad is an indescribable experience. From throwing house parties for two weeks straight to winning step shows, to the road trips, community service, and the impact that we had on the yard, let's just say you had to be there to really understand.

Senior year, I was a big fish in a little pond. I was Jahliel Thurman, SGA President, Nu Psi Chapter Basileus, party promoter, and host for some campus events. I even gave a speech at graduation; normally, it is just the class president. When I got to the podium, some of my classmates greeted me, screaming in a high-pitched voice, "*Juice! Juice! Juice! Juice!*" At that moment, I realized I had a true impact on people in college, and for me, that was extremely satisfying. However, that is not the end of the story.

Today I am a full-time entrepreneur. I have a digital marketing company called Yard Talk 101 that works within the HBCU space in order to help provide positive exposure and to increase awareness for HBCUs. I am an executive producer and host of my own show on AspireTV called *HBCU 101*. HBCU 101 is a show that highlights the culture, lifestyle and entertainment of HBCUs. I am also a mental health advocate. Having a strong mind is extremely essential to navigating life.

Virginia State University prepared me in ways in which I did not understand while in college. Being in SGA helped me to understand how to connect with presidents and other officials at other campuses while trying to grow my business from ground up. Joining a fraternity assisted me in gaining a skill set and a network that is unmatched. Being a mass communications major and hosting events helped me learn how to connect with crowds and with people on camera. Party promoting taught me how to hustle on a business level.

VSU taught me how to adapt in any environment, so much so that I took a leap of faith to move from Richmond to Atlanta to chase the dream of becoming a television host. Virginia State University adopted me when I was kid trying to understand life and groomed me into the adult I am today. Because of that, Virginia State University will forever have my heart. Thank you, VSU.

About Jahliel Thurman

"Success is failure after failure, without the loss of enthusiasm!" That is a quote by Winston Churchill that rising star Jahliel Thurman lives by.

Jahliel Thurman, a Chicago native, was born on April 7, 1992, to Yolanda and Malcohm Thurman. At a young age, it was evident that Mr. Thurman was destined for success! With both parents pushing him towards academic excellence, while introducing him to new and different cultures; it's safe to say they were grooming a unique individual.

Throughout his life, Jahliel has always succeeded, not only in the classroom but also with extracurricular activities. After graduating high school with honors, he was granted a full academic scholarship to the Virginia State University. During his undergraduate tenure, Jahliel served as President of the Student Government Association, President of the Nu Psi Chapter of Omega Psi Phi Fraternity, Incorporated. In addition to balancing other leadership positions within various academic organizations. Just like a footprint, Jahliel has left his permanent mark on the campus of Virginia State University.

On May 11, 2014, Jahliel was blessed to receive his Bachelors of Arts in Mass Communications with his concentration in Television and Broadcasting. With his love for HBCUs combined with a desire to broadcast the positivity amongst those institutions, Yard Talk 101 was born.

Yard Talk 101 strives to serve as the platform to exhibit the talents, programs, community projects, helpful resources, as well as other successes of fellow HBCU students and alumnus. With the future of Yard Talk 101 looking extremely promising, Jahliel is constantly working with other brands to help elevate the HBCU community and show them in the positive light they were all meant to be represented in. Today, Yard Talk 101 can be found on Aspire TV's digital platform.

Jahliel is determined to not let anything stand in his way while on this journey saying, " When we are going through rough times, remember we are not the only ones who have been down this path; someone before you had to overcome those adversities, so why to can't we?"

ASSEMBLYMAN BENJIE E. WIMBERLY

The Legacy Continues
Assemblyman Benjie E. Wimberly

My HBCU experience has taught me the true definition of legacy. Although the dictionary defines legacy as materialistic or monetary items that you leave behind, my experiences at Virginia State University showed me that legacy is about the impact one leaves behind.

Many moons ago, I embarked on my journey at Virginia State University, not knowing that VSU would be a home away from the home that I'd always known in Paterson, New Jersey. Growing up in Paterson wasn't easy. In fact, I learned many hard life lessons through friends who I watched fall victim to the streets, to prison, to drug addictions and early deaths. I vowed to myself, and to my praying mother, that my story wouldn't end that way. Virginia State University (VSU) gave me that opportunity to keep my promise. It allowed me to build a foundation on excellence, leadership, service, responsibility, truth and legacy.

I received so much more than a bachelor's degree in sociology at VSU. Learning about my history and roots on a collegiate level gave me the perspective that I needed to understand the importance of my presence as a black man in America. It was at VSU that I met many of my peers who were just as smart, talented and passionate as I was. I've gained role models and mentors through my professors and other VSU faculty members. The friendships and bonds that I developed are lifelong. I was also intiated into the Nu Psi Chapter of Omega Psi Phi Fraternity, Inc. at VSU, where I inherited a host of brothers and mentors. Through this brotherhood and many friendships, I learned the importance of family and accountability. My brothers and sisters at VSU challenged me to hold myself accountable and demanded a level of excellence in all areas of my life. My HBCU experience gave me the humility that's crucial when working in public service. It's the compassion I need to serve, and the confidence I need to lead.

15

The lessons, experiences and bonds I gained at VSU motivated me to return to my city and make a difference. Upon graduating, I served as a special education teacher in Paterson, as a baseball head coach, football head coach and a councilman at-large for the City of Paterson.

I served on the City of Paterson's Department of Public Works Committee, Public Safety Committee, Finance Committee, Health and Human Services Committee and Statutory Agencies Committee.

I am currently a New Jersey State Assemblyman, representing the 35th Legislative District. I was appointed deputy speaker and I serve as chairman on the Assembly Housing and Community Development Committee. Additionally, I am a member of the Assembly Budget Committee, member of the Assembly Transportation and Independent Authorities Committee, co-chair on the Joint Committee on Economic Justice and Equal Employment Opportunity, executive member on the New Jersey State Interscholastic Athletic Association (NJSIAA), member of the New Jersey State Employment & Training Commission, the Intergovernmental Relations Commission and the Commission to Review Constructive Sentences of Life Imprisonment on Juvenile Offenders.

In addition to my job as a state legislator, I am head football coach for Hackensack High School, the recreation director for the City of Paterson, a devoted husband of a fellow VSU alum, and a proud dad of four amazing young men—one who currently attends VSU.

VSU has passed down the true concept of legacy to me. It's not about titles or accolades. It's not about material items or monetary gain. It's about the impact you have on others. Helping people and restoring hope within my community has been my legacy for the last 30+ years, and VSU has played a major role in shaping the person I am today.

I am proud to say that my two oldest sons have embarked upon their own HBCU experience, and my third son will soon join the club this fall. It is my hope that my sons understand my legacy and leave behind a legacy of their own.

About Assemblyman Benjie E. Wimberly

Benjie E. Wimberly, was elected Assemblyman of the New Jersey 35th Legislative District in November of 2011 and was just re-elected November 2019 for his 5th Term. He currently serves as the Deputy Speaker and sits on the Assembly Budget Committee, Chairman of the Housing & Community Development Committee and Transportation and Independent Authorities Committee, the Joint Committee on Housing Affordability, the Joint Committee on the Public Schools and Co-Chairman of the Joint Committee on Economic Justice and Equal Employment Opportunity. NJ General Assembly Speaker has also appointed him to serve on the NJSIAA (New Jersey State Interscholastic Athletic Association and the NJSETC (New Jersey State Employment & Training Commission). He has previously served as the Chairman of the Commerce & Economic Development Committee, Vice Chairman of Telecommunications & Utilities Committee, Vice Chairman of the Assembly Regulatory Oversight and Reform and Federal Relations Committee, the Assembly Judiciary Committee and the Assembly Women & Children Committee.

He is a 1989 graduate of Virginia State University, where he earned a bachelor's degree in sociology. He holds a certificate as a teacher of children with disabilities from William Paterson University. He is the recreation coordinator for Paterson Public Schools and the head football coach for Hackensack High School. He previously was head football coach at Paterson Catholic High School.

Mr. Wimberly is a life member of Omega Psi Phi Fraternity Inc., a member of the NAACP and Rev. Frank Napier, Jr. Scholarship Committee, as well as many boards and commissions. Mr. Wimberly has collaborated with his civic organization, TEAM HOPE, council colleagues and community agencies to provide the following services: expungements seminars, tax appeal seminars, foreclosure workshops, go green initiatives, clothing drives, dinner for the needy, toy drives, Project Graduation, Thanksgiving turkey donations and community clean ups, as well as the Jordan Cleaves Scholarship Fund.

Additionally, Assemblyman Wimberly has been recognized with many awards, citations, proclamations, resolutions ... to name a few. In 2017, he received a Lifetime Achievement Award presented by President Barack Obama.

Assemblyman Wimberly and his wife Kimberlynn are proud parents of four sons: Justin, Jared, Jordan, and Jaden.

JERMAINE "JELLY" SIMPSON

Legendary

Jermaine "Jelly" Simpson

I am a native of the south side of Chicago. My mother and father moved my brother and I to Virginia, where I have lived for over twenty years. I attended Prince George High School, where I received my diploma, along with many awards for my military (Junior ROTC) and athletic achievements. Numerous colleges showed interest in my football abilities. I decided on Virginia State University (VSU) based on the trusted words of my soon-to-be mentor, Michael Shackleford.

When I first got to VSU, I was nervous and didn't know what to expect. I just knew not to step on the Trojan head by Foster Hall. I was "the man" in high school. Somehow, I knew that wouldn't be the case at VSU. When it came to football, I was surrounded by guys who were bigger and faster. But that only built up my motivation to work harder to compete with them. I went to my ROTC mentor, Sargent Thomas, to ask him what I could do to get faster and stronger. He not only put my physical body to the test, but my mental body, as well. Little did I know, ROTC would become the backbone of my wellbeing throughout my VSU experience.

Through my hard work with ROTC, I soon became a ranger. I made some great friends who became my fraternity brothers in The National Society of Pershing Rifles, Oscar 4 Company. Through my hard work, I finally got the opportunity to show what I could do on the field by starting at outside linebacker. I was happy, nervous and scared all at once because I didn't want to lose my spot. It's hard to get the starting job, but even harder to keep it.

In my latter years at VSU, I grew into my own and became an influence on campus within the student body and the administration. I became a student ambassador.

I hosted functions around campus and one group of men stood out to me in a positive way. I went to my mentor, Dr. Shackleford, who shared

21

their same principles. He provided me with guidance and wisdom, and told me the things to do in order to become a member. This organization was the men of Omega Psi Phi Fraternity, Inc.

After a lot of hard work and dedication, juggling schoolwork, football and ROTC, I was blessed and fortunate enough to cross in the spring of 2000 Nu Psi Chapter and became sergeant at arms. After showing my allegiance to the chapter, and displaying hard work, I was voted by my peers to be dean of the spring 2002 line.

While at VSU, I showed leadership skills, teamwork and balance. I achieved much notoriety and respect for my contribution to the university, such as the VSU Unsung Hero 2002. I joined five organizations at Virginia State University. I served as captain, defensive end and defensive tackle on the Virginia State Football Team. I joined the National Society of Pershing Rifles Oscar-4 as sergeant at arms; Omega Psi Phi Fraternity, Incorporated, Nu Psi Chapter as an active member; and the sergeant at arms and dean to the spring 2002 line of the chapter. I was also a student ambassador for three years and ROTC Trojan Warrior Battalion. Upon completion of my bachelor's degree at Virginia State University, I had the opportunity to attend the NFL Combine, where The New York Jets picked me up. However, due to a knee injury, I wasn't able to complete training camp with the team.

I attended Virginia Commonwealth University (VCU) to receive my master's in sports management. I, along with my best friend, Ronnie Neal, was able to develop a promotions company based on the social presence we had at the university. The company, Uplift Entertainment, created a buzz around the university and among other schools, such as Virginia State University and Virginia Union University. We were able to establish a team of students to help move the company forward in an uplifting way, such as providing scholarships and donations throughout the school year. The company is still active today.

After completing my master's degree, I used my abilities to land a job as sales manager at a well-known car dealership know as Nissan of Mechanicsville. I demonstrated my ability to give back to the university with my company and provide additional financial support from Sheehy Nissan.

I was still passionate about furthering my education after I graduated. I decided to add The Emergency Preparedness Program to my resume. I earned a certificate in Emergency Preparedness from VCU. I worked for VSU for a period as resident educator and made an impact on the students who stayed in Seward Hall. I served as the director of the Residence Life and earned the Hall of the Year Honors. With the education I received from the Emergency Preparedness Program, I was able to put in place policies and procedures to help with residence life.

I later returned to the car business as a sales Manager for Nissan of Mechanicsville. I continued to work at the promotional company, Uplift Entertainment, in addition to my work at the dealership. I made a positive name for myself throughout the nightclub scene. During this time, I met my soon-to-be wife, Natalie Simpson, while working on a business deal to collaborate with her company. Natalie and I have established a clothing line, Uplift Clothing Apparel, to promote uplifting experiences through clothing. We are both active in the church community at The Life Church. If I'm not working at the dealership on a Sunday, I'm at church providing services as security and overseer while I receive the Word of the Lord.

My experience at VSU was something I will never forget. When this kid from Chicago stepped on that yard, I made a lasting impression—not only to myself—but to the numerous classmates, friends and teammates I encountered. I cherished every minute at VSU, and I love it.

About Jermaine "Jelly" Simpson

Jermaine Simpson is a 2002 graduate from Virginia State University. After graduating Jermaine received an opportunity to try out with the New York Jets, but that was short lived after suffering a knee injury causing him to come back to Virginia to further his education. While pursuing his Master's Degree at VCU, Jermaine and VSU grad Ronnie Neal took their love for cultivating events and connecting people and they founded Uplift Entertainment, a promotional group catering towards events in Richmond and DC area. Later in early 2018, Jermaine and wife Natalie Simpson created Uplift Clothing Apparel, which is a fun and exciting clothing brand based on 90's and 2000's TV shows and movies with a touch of school spirit.

KENYANA YATES

A Different World

Kenyana Yates

I grew up entrenched in all cultures globally, thanks to my parents. So, adapting to diverse environments was second nature for me. Prior to high school, I knew I wanted to delve into one of two professions: a medical doctor or an engineer. The type of school I would attend never crossed my mind until my freshman year of high school when I had the opportunity to take my first Introduction to Engineering class. That's when I discussed what HBCUs were with my family. Initially, I had scholarship offers to attend everywhere except an HBCU. That's when the college tours began that forever changed the trajectory of my adult life.

Virginia State University (VSU) was not my first choice. Ironically, Howard University and North Carolina A&T were. My mother jokingly told me that I was too "green" for Howard. Although I verbally disagreed, I knew she was right. When I got accepted to A&T, the finances didn't align when I weighed my options against in-state schools that I had partial scholarships to attend. It was hard to debate with my parents against the idea of leaving school with no debt versus the out-of-state offerings.

Visiting each of those campuses was the dose of empowerment that I needed. Sometimes, the challenge with growing up in diverse environments was that the experience away from home was that I was the only one who looked like me in a lot of arenas. Even in the engineering college-prep classes, I was *different*. I yearned for a new experience.

VSU was one of my last college tour stops. I hopped out of the car and literally felt like I had stepped into a different world. By then, I knew engineering was my path, but I didn't know if VSU offered it in their curriculum. The campus was immaculate. I know we don't lay blankets on the yard in between classes, but I was legitimately ready to be that nerd who did just that. It was perfect and just far enough away from home to feel independent. The culture was so rich. Ironically, the incoming group of budding engineers on the tour was diverse. But, for the first time, I wasn't the only one. That was empowering. After the tour, I literally felt like there was nothing that I couldn't do.

My first encounter on campus was with a room full of freshman girls and empowering black women from Delta Sigma Theta Sorority, Inc., Alpha Eta Chapter. They gave us *real* feedback on how to conduct ourselves as ladies on campus. Little did I know that they would one day become my big sisters. Their words of wisdom and warnings stuck with me. I did not ever fathom that college was a place that some people could lose sight of their goals. However, it was there that I learned the resilience to not let your distractions alter your course of success.

My freshman year, I was off to the races—but not literally. The hardest decision I had to make that year was to not run track. I had cross-country scholarships from other schools. But, at VSU, my scholarships were academic-based. I loved track and field, so not doing it was not easy. I had been running nearly year-round since I was a child. It was at that point that I knew I was not going to the Olympics, which was a prior goal. So, I retired my spikes and headed to the basement of Fauntleroy for one of my first engineering classes. Back then, we didn't have a beautiful, sprawling engineering building next to the café. We had the basement.

That location is where we cultivated some of the greatest lifelong connections with people who wanted to make it. And we wanted to do it *together*. I had a professor who proclaimed that not all of us would make it. He was right. But then, there was Dr. Thompkins. He was a Caucasian male who wanted us to thrive. He challenged us and wouldn't let us give up. He e-mailed me over the summer to see how I was doing, and he helped me get my first internship. That is what made being at an HBCU different. Everyone wanted to see me succeed, no matter their nationality.

Throughout my first two years, I was strategic about the activities I was involved in on campus. I joined The National Society of Black Engineers, serving on the freshman council.

By my senior year, I'd become the first Region 2 O-Zone Coordinator from Virginia State, representing every college in the state of Virginia. I was also a member of The American Society of Mechanical Engineers and the pep club. Let's just say I knew I was not extroverted enough to continue hollering at games, but the pep club was a definite Trojan pride booster. My identity was still taking shape, so I thought I needed balance between the nerdy activities and those that weren't academically based.

Sophomore year, I joined the Virginia State University Gospel Chorale (VSUGC) and Kerojo Modeling Agency, LTD. I had modeled and sang overseas and stateside for fun, but this was another level. The sheer confidence the upper classmen had as they hit the runway was astounding. Having that confidence in my toolkit would aid me in the near future as I walked into corporations for job interviews.

My final year of school, a group of us got together and chartered Tau Alpha Pi Engineering Honor Society. That literally made me feel like I could accomplish anything.

VSU was not a school that was widely known for engineering, but I was determined to open as many doors as I possibly could for those coming behind me. As I interviewed for jobs against "giants" from other schools like M.I.T., Clemson and Cornell, I didn't lack any confidence that I could compete equally. Even with the most condescending interviewers who were vocal about whether I could measure up, my combined experience at VSU, and the shoulders of the people I stood upon, didn't allow me to waiver in my expectations of achieving greatness.

My HBCU experience helped mold me into the person I am today. It further reinforced that, with faith and perseverance, there is nothing I can't accomplish. VSU showed me what pride looked like among the masses. Being different made each of us amazing forces to be reckoned with. When we came together, we were unstoppable.

"Forth we go to the world to do service. Thy lofty command to fulfill; with thy light, go dispel all darkness and thus do the Father's will."

Hail, State!

About Kenyana R. Yates

Kenyana was born in Columbia, SC and raised in Virginia Beach, VA. As a product of a military family she has lived around the world.

She graduated with honors from VSU with a degree in Mechanical Engineering Technology in 2004. Utilizing the engineering training and leadership skills learned while in school, she continued to challenge the status quo, and currently serves as a Senior Leader in the Nation's largest Internet Retail Company globally.

After VSU Kenyana continued her studies through Downline Ministries Institute, an intensive training program committed to equipping men and women from all backgrounds in biblical history and discipleship; she later answered the *call* to become an ordained minister.

In the community Kenyana continues to seize the opportunity to serve through multiple platforms including Delta Sigma Theta Sorority, Incorporated, where she pledged through the Alpha Eta Chapter. She also helped charter Tau Alpha Pi Engineering Honor Society while on campus. Kenyana went on to serve as an Auxiliary Board Member for United Way, Habitat for Humanity volunteer, and a co-founder of S.T.R.E.N.G.T.H Teen Ministry.

Separately, she has been recognized for her work in Diversity Careers in Engineering and Who's Who. However, her most notable accomplishment is raising two beautiful girls with her husband.

DR. MICHAEL RAINEY

The Potter and the Clay

Dr. Michael L. Rainey, Ed.D.

And to think...it could've been over with the snap of my fingers.

Just like that!

I was a high school senior. I was filling out two to five applications a week to find money wherever I could. I filled out college applications, any and every local, state, and national opportunity on Fastweb, and more. I randomly received a packet in the mail the first week in January of 1998. Feeling overwhelmed, I said to myself, "Enough is enough!" I threw the packet in the trash and went on with life, partly because I was over filling out applications. I knew there was no way I would be selected. A week later, I was watching *Coming to America* for the umpteenth time when the line, "Go on honey, take a chance!" was uttered during that iconic train scene. In that moment, I fished the packet out of the trash with two days to spare for the postmark deadline.

About three months later, I received a call asking to set up a phone interview, which occurred a few days afterward. Three weeks later, Ms. Sheila Milburn from the United States Department of Agriculture took the stage at Carver High School's Class Day to announce that I had received the USDA/1890 National Scholarship, which constituted a full scholarship, computer and an annual summer internship in a fully-furnished apartment in Washington, D.C. starting that summer. I headed to the busy city alone two weeks after graduation. I also had a guaranteed job with the USDA upon college graduation. To this day, I can't believe it. I actually *threw this opportunity away* because I doubted myself and I was being lazy about completing yet another application. I never would have imagined not only being one of 32 students selected nationally, but being the top scholar assigned to USDA Headquarters. And to think...it could've been over with the snap of my fingers. *Just like that!*

I initially received the North Carolina Teaching Fellows Scholarship at UNC at Chapel Hill and a partial scholarship for NC State University. The

33

USDA/1890 National Scholarship offered me the opportunity to attend any of the seventeen land grant institutions in the country. Being from Winston-Salem, I didn't want to go to NC A&T State University since I hadn't been that impressed from a previous tour. Plus, many people from my high school were going there. So, I decided on Virginia State University. It wasn't too far from home if I needed to get to my parents, or vice versa. Plus, my aunt lived in Virginia Beach. Because of my internship at USDA, I missed the opportunities for orientations and touring campus. However, after my parents picked me up from D.C. at the conclusion of the internship, we stopped through campus on the way home. Once we drove onto campus, I instantly knew that VSU was home and that I had made the right decision.

I immediately sought out ways to get involved. I joined various organizations like The Walter Johnson Mathematics Club, NC Pre-Alumni Association and the Minorities in Agriculture, Natural Resources, and Related Sciences (MANRRS). I made some wonderful friends and began forging pivotal relationships with faculty and staff members from the onset. All was going well, until I learned later in the semester that the school was withholding many of my scholarships from my refund check because I had too many. Apparently, in this unpublicized policy, there was a cap on the amount of financial aid a student could receive, which was a little over $16,000. Well, I already had a full scholarship. I was a Presidential Scholar (in name only since I had a full scholarship) and an Institute for Leadership Development Scholar (again, in name only). Additionally, I had about $10,000 in local and state scholarships. If checks were made directly to me (which they weren't), then I would've been good. So, imagine to the surprise of my parents and me when all that money was gone! Even checks made out to both the school and me jointly, including the $3,500 from my dad's job, was all gone! Just because I didn't have a balance with the school didn't mean I didn't need that money. I had basic expenses like food, toiletries and gas. I had worked hard to earn every penny awarded to me. The school's response was nothing but this crazy policy. At the time, they had never seen a student come through VSU with the amount of scholarships I had. This was new territory for them.

I made up my mind over Christmas break, declaring, "Y'all ain't gonna screw me over and think it's okay!" I put in my transfer request to my second choice for placement and submitted my admissions application to NC A&T (remember, my scholarship was good for seventeen schools). I was prepared to say goodbye to Virginia State University after freshman year. Then, something magical happened.

I heard about auditions for the VSU Gospel Chorale. Out of all my initial experiences at VSU, joining the chorale was the most rewarding and engaging. It kept me connected to church. And, as a choir director and musician, I didn't have to worry about being in charge. I could just "be." I'd never seen or heard a choir like this. The dynamic singing, the choreography, the robes and the outfits were second to none. During the spring semester, I also connected with Ms. Lisa Wynn, the director of admissions at the time. She took me under her wing and allowed me to volunteer in the office. She even let me travel with her back to my hometown to help recruit at the CIAA Basketball Tournament and by myself at my old high school. Truth be told, it was the choir and this opportunity with Ms. Wynn that kept me at VSU.

VSU continued to birth new things within me, literally molding me into the man I am today. In fact, I would like to think VSU was the potter, and I was the clay. Attending VSU allowed me to join Kappa Alpha Psi Fraternity, Inc., to lead the best college gospel choir as its treasurer and president, be part of an amazing family experience, receive some amazing mentors, and make lifelong friends. In May of 2002, VSU birthed a valedictorian who was able to compete with predominantly white institution graduates to receive a full scholarship from Wake Forest University and secure a job with the U.S. Army as a research analyst. VSU has been such a blessing.

I've served as an advisor for my undergraduate fraternity chapter since 2005, in which it has been recognized at, and received accolades on, the province and national levels. I have also worked for VSU's Department of Student Activities as its assistant coordinator for Leadership Development, leading The Royal Court, Student Government Association and Freshman

Class Council. I've worked in the music department as the business operations director for the VSU Gospel Chorale for a number of years, and as an instructor for First Year Experience.

Because of the leadership opportunities I had as a student, and those afforded to me beyond graduation, I've had the pleasure of helping countless students realize their potential. I've left a legacy through the creation of meaningful programs, policies and initiatives, and I've been instrumental in a lot of campus "firsts," such as appearing on *America's Got Talent* or collaborating with Food Lion to establish a campus food pantry to fight food insecurity.

My association with VSU, and the work I've done beyond college, has allowed me to become the program coordinator for CIAA's Education Day and Career Expo and coordinator for the Miss CIAA Scholarship Competition. Because of the interest I had in education, and the love I had for helping children and young adults realize their potential, I obtained my doctorate degree in education. What better place to take this journey than to drink from the fountain of knowledge, yet again at VSU?

Now, my devotion and commitment allow me to operate as one of VSU's biggest cheerleaders. My commitment to VSU has not only afforded me the opportunity to be an active member of the VSU Alumni Association, but I'm proud to serve as its national vice-president to help preserve the ideals, traditions and rich history of VSU, while giving back and uplifting our students.

VSU is not just a place to receive the education of your life. It's also a place where one can dream, explore and succeed while being a part of a transformative experience. Life has been amazing. I couldn't imagine my life without VSU. It seems so surreal. God knew what He was doing when I went back to the trash that day.

And to think...it could've been over with the snap of my fingers.

Just like that.

About Dr. Michael L. Rainey, Ed.D.

Michael L. Rainey graduated as the 2002 valedictorian from Virginia State University with a B.S. in Mathematics with double concentrations in Computer Science and Mathematics Education. He went on to receive his M.A. in Mathematics from Wake Forest University in 2004 and his doctorate in Educational Administration and Supervision in 2019 from Virginia State University. Professionally, he is an operations research analyst with the U.S. Army and a Freshman Studies instructor at Virginia State University.

Rainey is a 2001 initiate of Alpha Phi (E) Chapter of Kappa Alpha Psi Fraternity, Inc., where he is also a life member. He is also an active and devoted alumnus of the University. He has managed the VSU Gospel Chorale since 2008, chartered the VSUGC Chapter of the VSU Alumni Association in 2015, where he currently serves as president. He currently serves as the national vice-president, and is a life member, of the VSU Alumni Association.

CRYSTAL BOYD

Young, Gifted and Black

Crystal Boyd

I am a first-generation college graduate. Obtaining my degree was one of the best decisions I've ever made—not only the degree, but the institution I chose.

As a teenager from Brooklyn, New York, and attending the great Martin Luther King, Jr. High School, I always wanted greatness. I always wanted better for myself. I realize I wanted to go somewhere, not where I was tolerated, but where I could be accepted.

Once I chose the path of higher education, I didn't really know a lot about historically black colleges and universities. However, I knew I needed to go somewhere where I had opportunities to grow and be successful. I was accepted to quite a few schools, more than I expected actually. I knew I wanted to go away, but I wasn't sure where I wanted to go. Virginia State University was my final pick due to location.

The Virginia State University experience is unique. To be a Trojan is to be one-of-a-kind. I gained an extended family at VSU. No matter where you go, you can always find a Trojan welcoming you with open arms. I was able to gain friends and family from places I only knew of from the map. I learned life lessons and went through many obstacles. It all helped me become a better version of myself. Sometimes, I felt like it wasn't worth it. But the culture and campus life helped me turn the negatives to positives. VSU helped me remember that success is failure turned inside out. With a strong support system, I made it through. VSU helped me grow and develop in a way that groomed me for the world today. I experienced real-life situations that helped me in my adult life. Brooklyn taught me the foundation of life; VSU showed me *how to use* that foundation. I am forever grateful for that.

VSU allowed me to go to the place Alfred William Harris dreamed of: "Where all may go and drink from the fountain of knowledge until their ambition is satiated." This quote, located at The Fountain, was forever embedded in me. The amount of knowledge and history I had access to was beyond comprehension. I didn't just obtain a degree; I increased in knowledge of historical information just for the fact that my university is located in the Mecca of black history. Many black history facts that we learned about in books are right in the area of my beloved campus.

At the home of fraternities and countless social organizations, I embarked upon a journey that was one of a kind. I joined a social organization because I had a strong passion to help others. I also wanted to get familiar with the local community I was going to be in for the next four years.

Becoming a member of the newly created student organization founded in 2007, The Student Liaison Outreach Team (S.L.O.T.) was another special experience. I gained forever family and friends and excelled my verbal and writing communication skills. My love of writing took off. Now, 13 years later and 200+ members, S.L.O.T. is still thriving and living the mission that I helped started. I was only in it for the mission, but it opened doors that money can't buy, and that, is priceless.

Once on campus, I shortly figured out my major. Because of all the things happening on campus, I caught myself gravitating toward the mass communications club events. I craved knowledge and wanted to learn in a new, exciting way. As a mass communications major, it offered me more opportunities, such as writing for *The Statesman* and other local companies in the area. I went on to write for a *Fortune 500* company.

VSU had iconic building names after prominent alumni, such as Reginald Lewis, former owner of TLC Beatrice International; William H. Lewis, the first African-American Assistant Attorney General; James Avery, actor; Billy Taylor, jazz musician; and Dr. Mary Hatwood Futrell, former president of the National Education Association. This was even more intriguing because I know that people who look like me did extraordinary things. That let me know I could do extraordinary things as well. There are no limits here. And there are no limits at VSU.

I am beyond satisfied that I picked VSU. It was all I expected, and then some.

I am a proud Trojan daughter of the school on the hill. I am VSUMADE.

About Crystal Boyd

Crystal Jewel Boyd now Davis one of five siblings and is a native of Brooklyn, New York

An alumna of The Virginia State University, class of May 2008 and obtained Bachelor of Arts Communication, a concentration Public Relations and a minor in English.

A proud Charter Member of The Student Liaison Outreach Program, one of the best decisions she ever made besides going to college. Boyd gained knowledge of starting and running a non-profit organization and a special passion for community service and helping children in the local area.

A current Entrepreneur, currently a liaison on assisting others to open businesses and owner of Jewelz Distrikt. These two entities allow her to help others and see significant changes occur. A member of Order of Eastern Star allows her to do community service work & build sisterhood in her spare time.

Married her College Sweetheart, Robert Davis IV and they share a teacup yorkie, Ace.

JEROME HOOD

The Yard Legend

Jerome Hood

In the 90s, I grew up in New Jersey. My uncle used to host a bus trip to the Meadowlands (NY Giants Stadium). We'd all gather and go watch Howard and Hampton play in the Labor Day Classic. At the time, I was only eleven years old, so I didn't know the significance of an HBCU. I didn't even know what an HBCU was at the time. We would arrive at the game to see our people in an area tailgating, partying, socializing and having a great time before the game. The chatter was always about the game's halftime show. The bands would step on the field in their freshest garments and play the latest hip-hop or R&B song to dazzle the crowd. It was the most amazing thing I'd ever seen.

During my senior year in high school, I sat in my coach's office, talking about life after high school. At that time, I didn't even know if my heart was fully into staying in New Jersey or playing college basketball; however, I knew I wanted to go to college and play basketball. I was one foot in, one foot out. I visited a few schools, but I wasn't blown away by anything they had to offer.

One Sunday, we had a meeting at one of our local organization offices. They announced that they were giving an HBCU tour. The schools included VA Union, Virginia State University (VSU), Bowie and Hampton University. I immediately signed up for it. On the college tour, the day we stepped foot on Virginia State University was a hot day. Students were hanging out around the campus, and music was blasting from cars as they rode up and down the boulevard. One fraternity was stepping and doing their chants, while the girls and spectators watched. The energy, the vibration and atmosphere were electrifying. It was a sea of beautiful black people. From that moment, I knew I wanted to attend VSU.

As soon as I got back home, I told my mother that I wanted to apply to VSU. Forgetting everything that was on the table from other schools who had recruited me for basketball, I'd made my mind up. I applied to VSU in

2004 and got accepted. I couldn't believe I was going all the way to Virginia from New Jersey to attend school. No family, no friends and no support system. I was just a young kid on a mission.

My five years (don't laugh; I was on a five-year plan) at Virginia State University were a blast. My first year at VSU was all about partying and meeting people. I knew from jump that I wanted to connect with people. I didn't want to be an anti-social person. I met people from New York, Los Angeles, Texas and Florida. I met people from anywhere you could name or think of. Freshman year was a big party. During my freshman year, BET's *College Hill* was filming. It was a movie on "the yard," a nickname for our campus. We would go to class, then hit the yard and chill out all day until the sun goes down. We created memories while hanging on the yard. That's where legends are born.

Being a "Yard Legend" is hard work on and off campus. If you held it down and made the best of your experience while you were in school, you're a Yard Legend. The yard is where we all came together every day, no matter where you was from. The yard was the stage like in the movie, *Paid in Full.* One of my most memorable experiences was attending homecoming. Homecoming is where all the fellow alumni come back for the weekend and party. Seeing our people come together, young and old, and have a great time together, was truly breathtaking. We went around to different tailgates and tents. The older alumni showed love and the game was truly inspiring.

After my first year at Virginia State University, I quickly learned that college wasn't just all about partying. I really buckled down and understood the importance of attending VSU. The biggest thing I've learned was being able to network and build relationships. My biggest accomplishment, outside of graduating, was involving myself with different school organizations. Not only was I involved in S.L.OT., I also joined Phi Beta Sigma Fraternity, Inc. Joining a fraternity really showed me the meaning of brotherhood, family-oriented environment and networking.

Attending VSU was the best decision I've made in life. My HBCU experience was one for the books. The culture, history and the values of attending an HBCU cannot be compared to any other institution of higher learning. I like to use the phrase, "NJ raised me, but VA made me!" Virginia State University made me the man I am today. From the time I stepped foot on campus, I could tell it was a real close-knit, family-oriented environment. We had our trials and tribulations, and our ups and our downs. We had our arguments, our fights and our deaths. However, I can really say that VSU is a family and we always come out on top.

No matter where I am in the world, if someone I know lives in or has ties to a certain area, I can call them and they will make sure I'm straight. I may not have even known them at school; however, we make sure that we take care of our fellow Trojans. Without attending Virginia State University, I don't know where I'd be. I don't know who I would have become. As an alum, I want to be the one who shows the younger generation love at homecoming. Legends are made at HBCU's all across the land. However, only Yard Legends are made at VSU.

About Jerome Hood

Jerome Hood was born and raised in Somerville, New Jersey. He graduated from Virginia State University (Petersburg, VA) in 2009 with a Bachelor's in Business Marketing. Mr. Hood later obtained a Masters in Education Management from Strayer University (Richmond, VA). While attending the prestigious Virginia State University, he became a man of Phi Beta Sigma Fraternity Inc, Tri Alpha Chapter.

Jerome Hood is a serial entrepreneur and over the year's have grown some of his endeavors to multimillion dollar business. Jerome Hood serves as the Chief Executive Officer/ Co Founder of Bridging The Gap Family Services, Chief Executive Officer/ Founder of Pushing Our Cultural Forward Publishing, Chairman/Co Founder of The Ville Legacy Leadership Foundation (Non Profit 503c) and also a Real Estate Investor.

Bridging the Gap Family Services provides quality and reputable counseling for youth and their families, with emotional, behavioral and mental health challenges. Licensed by the Virginia Department of Behavioral Health and Development Services and credentialed by Magellan of Virginia, our company is committed to serving at-risk individuals and families of Virginia.

Pushing Our Culture Forward Publishing is a reputable publishing company in which provides content geared towards uplifting and educating our culture. POCFP creates content through books, web channels, and short films.

The Ville Legacy Leadership Foundation is a 501 (C) 3 non-profit organization established in Jerome's hometown to bridge the gap between various generations in an effort to address the needs of our communities. Our goal is to provide quality outreach events within the communities we serve. We are committed to breaking the vicious cycle of stereotypes formed from generation after generation.

Jerome Hood loves to extend a helping hand to further the advancement of his peers. Jerome Hood looks to expand his empire and get into Venture Capital tech startups. It is a goal of Jerome Hood to open up a co-working center in his hometown in the near future.

NATAN MCKENZIE

Councilman

Natan Mckenzie

Growing up, my childhood was *almost* typical. I grew up in a Jamaican and Dominican household, with five brothers and sisters. We moved between five different houses and states before I reached ninth grade. I also experienced six different school systems. Needless to say, connecting with my peers was always a challenge. No one could relate with my background. And those who could, were few and far between. So, when it came to choosing a college, I wanted to experience what it meant to live and learn amongst people who would view me as I was, not for whom they thought *I was supposed to be.*

From the moment I stepped foot onto VSU's campus, my HBCU gave me the opportunity and resilience to become the man I am today. As a freshman, I participated in the freshman showcase, which gave me the strong lesson of resiliency. Facing an HBCU crowd for the first time as a freshman will do that to you. I also joined the Betterment of Brothers and Sisters organization, which gave me the foundation to conduct myself in a professional manner. It was an outlet to service my community, and I was exposed to the reason why every HBCU alum is really family after graduation, but rivals beforehand. As the years progressed, I pledged the Beta Gamma Chapter of Alpha Phi Alpha Fraternity, Inc., and graduated from the Reginald F. Lewis School of Business with my Bachelor of Science in marketing.

Thanks to the toughest teacher that I had, Dr. Sharma, I was introduced to the world of finance—and the shaking reality of how ignorant I was to it. I quickly realized that I wasn't the only one who was truly ignorant—at no fault of our own—to the world of finance. I wanted to change that fact deeply. I worked at a local bank as a teller while at VSU and personally witnessed the harsh reality of what being financially ignorant could lead to. It became evident to me that this was my passion.

I pursued a career that fit my passion as a financial advisor. Over the past ten years, I have worked with multiple companies and have helped hundreds of clients achieve a healthy financial lifestyle. I am now an independent financial advisor and a partner with Freedom Infinite Growth (FIG) Investments. FIG Investments is an investment club focused on financially funding our communities for and with our communities. We host financial educational courses to expose our community to a deeper understanding of the market and the foundations to a healthy financial lifestyle.

I have always wanted to help others—not just financially—but socioeconomically, as well. Everyone should have an equal chance at living a good life. I was living in Petersburg, Virginia during the time I studied at VSU. I got to know the community well and viewed it as another piece of my family. I also got to spend a lot of time servicing the community in the city of Petersburg. It lies within a food desert. There was not much economic progress outside of the tourism industry and restaurants. As I continued to search for solutions to the problems facing our community, and I partnered with various groups to ensure I was doing more than my part, I coached soccer for my local YMCA. I was a lecturer at my church and I served as a mentor with Big Brothers Big Sisters. I was a member of a local health organization, the Petersburg Wellness Consortium, and a member of the Urban League of Greater Richmond Young Professionals (YP). Although I was able to do what I could, I quickly noticed that it was going to take more than just me to solve these conditions that our community was facing economically, socially and environmentally.

During a tour of our state capital, I got the idea to run for office. I shared a conversation with a fellow Trojan—who was very politically motivated— about my desire to get into politics. That's when I first knew I could win an election and work toward building a better community. Shortly after this conversation, I formulated a strategy to run for city council in Petersburg in 2014. My campaign team mostly consisted of VSU Trojans, both alumni and the current student body. I also had the support of community members and local professionals. This was my first campaign for any election, let alone a public office. After countless meetings, knocking on doors, and greeting people, I finished second place. I had a tremendous race and I was able to show that anyone who has the drive, passion and vision for a better community can run for office and help change the world—one community at a time.

I continued to support my community in other ways. I became the executive director of the Restoration of Petersburg Community Development Corporation and instructed financial literacy courses for first-time homebuyers for the Latinos Economic Development Center in Washington, D.C. This was a trying period for me commuting back and forth. Before I knew it, 2018 was around the corner and that meant another shot at the election for city council. I ran again for the same city council seat. This time, I was a write-in candidate and needed to pull even more support because there were three additional candidates running for the same position. It was a more grassroots campaign. The VSU alumni and student body supported me up to the day of the election. We had a huge voter turnout and beat everyone, besides the incumbent with over 300 votes. It was something that I will always cherish. I look forward to doing it all again.

I have since continued to advance my career as a financial advisor working with FIG Investments. I also started my own photobooth business, Pix 'R Us, with my girlfriend. With her also being a wedding and event planner, we naturally do well in business with each other. We have already grown so much and have only been in business for a year. We have multiple photobooths and modern props, and we have secured multiple corporate contracts and just started taking on employees. There is no telling where our company will grow.

VSU has been nothing but a blessing to my life, my businesses and all my endeavors.

I cannot express how much gratitude I have for taking this road untraveled.

It truly made all the difference.

About Natan McKenzie

Natan McKenzie is a New Jersey born transplant currently living in Richmond, VA. He was a middle child in a family of eight and prides himself as a Afro-Latino with a Jamaican and Dominican heritage. Natan's journey has always been centered around his three major passions; Community Activism, Finance, and the Black Experience. This brought him to his beloved HBCU, Virginia State University. Upon completing his time at VSU he graduated with a BS in Marketing, received his Graduate certificate in Project Management, completed his CAPM certification, and pledged the Beta Gamma chapter of Alpha Phi Alpha Fraternity, inc. He went on to establish himself as a Financial Advisor/Advocate with over 10 years of experience, a partner with FIG Investments, ran for local political office, and is the co-owner of Pix R Us Photobooth. He strives to change the financial behaviors of his community, one client at a time.

JESSICA DREW

Gandy Hall

Jessica Drew

An alma mater, to some, may simply be a song for special occasions. I didn't realize the importance of the words and how much value it brought to my life until my full circle moment.

It started in the year 1991. I was two years old and my parents were full-time workers. Fortunately, my mom started a career at Virginia State University years prior after she graduated from the then college. Luckily for her, they offered on-campus childcare. My sister and I were enrolled at that daycare. I remember the hallways at the Center for Young Children and the basement of Gandy Hall. I can't say I didn't cry or fall out when my mom dropped me off for the day. I can say, however, that when I did, the teachers helped me gather my thoughts and have a great day!

I learned values, intellectual thought processing and interpersonal skills while being cared for at Virginia State University Center for Young Children. I graduated from the program and went on to kindergarten five miles away at Matoaca Elementary School. Somewhere between high school and deciding which college I wanted to attend, Virginia State University became my absolute last resort! I did *not* want to go to college at VSU. Not because of the school and its curricula, but because I literally lived there my entire life!

I had attended homecoming every year since I was ten years old. I'd participated in the homecoming parade since I was five years old. The phenomenal "Woo Woo Super Camps" exposed me to the student village and dormitory life before I'd even made it to middle school.

I even had dance recitals and award receptions when sports were complete on campus. I had seen enough of VSU and I wanted to venture out as a new high school graduate. I applied and was accepted to some elite universities. However, there's a popular saying: "Tell God your plans, and He will show you who the real plan maker is."

During my senior year of high school, I enrolled into a dual-trade program. This is a program where high school students learn a trade, become licensed and can begin working in the trade upon graduation. I was enrolled in the nursing program, which extended one year after graduation for licensure. This left me in a bind. All my friends were going away and starting their freshman year of college. I would be left behind in Matoaca, Virginia, all for an LPN license.

After discussing it with my parents, I determined that being able to work as a nurse while attending college wasn't a bad deal. The caveat was that I would enroll as a part-time student at Virginia State University in the fall of 2007, and transfer after the spring semester once my nursing program was completed. I didn't want to miss out on the "college right after high school" feeling that all my peers would experience. So, I enrolled at Virginia State University as a part-time, general education student in August of 2007.

I attended nursing school by day and classes at VSU by night. All was going well until my first homecoming as a university student. I stopped attending nursing school and enrolled full-time at VSU in the spring of 2008. As I parked on campus for spring registration, I looked up and there was Gandy Hall, the location where my VSU journey began. At that moment, I knew all was going to be okay. My future was bright. The culture, the comradery, the faculty and more pulled me in and helped break the stigma I had against attending VSU. So, here I was, enrolling full-time to the university I least wanted to attend. Matoaca is a small, homely village, where everyone knows everyone. So, matriculating through VSU could come as a shell shock.

During the 2008 semesters at VSU, I was introduced to Delta Sigma Theta Sorority, Incorporated and the numerous programs that the organization brought to the community.

In spring of 2009, I was afforded the opportunity to join the illustrious organization with 39 other college-educated women. Joining the sorority brought an abundance of opportunities to me during my collegiate years. I was most fortunate to create a bond that only these 39 ladies and I can relate to personally. Some of these girls became my best friends. In the spring 2010 semester, I ran for Miss Virginia State. This was my first time competing for a "title." Winning the competition was one of my greatest accomplishments while at VSU. The title was not to be taken lightly. I instantly became one of the major faces of the university, breaking the trend that previous university queens molded, in a good way of course.

As Miss Virginia State, I had several photo shoots. One of the mandatory locations I chose was the playground, which was still standing outside of Gandy Hall. The Miss VSU experience taught me ultimately how to create opportunity for others, as well as myself, by using my voice and platform. I take pride in the Miss Virginia State title and I still use the tools learned during that year to navigate through life. In December of 2011, I graduated from VSU with a double Bachelor of Science in Accounting and Management Information Systems. Now, my degrees allow me to see the world.

I share my alma mater with several thousand other graduates. But I am most proud to share the love of Virginia State University with my mom and my godmother. I continuously return to the university to give in any capacity. I encourage all Trojans to go back, but most importantly, to give back. Giving back isn't always financial. I will never forget all that my HBCU offered to me. I am forever grateful. From midnight breakfast gym jams and historic back lawn socials, to swag surfin' at the homecoming pep rally, Virginia State University was the college experience I wouldn't trade for the world.

I would have never thought I would value Virginia State University in the way that I do today. As I look back, it's funny how I literally began learning at VSU in 1991 and graduated with two degrees twenty years later. I am so glad I went to VSU and drank from the fountain of knowledge. I proudly wear my orange and blue! I proudly promote the history of my HBCU!

My alma mater and its lyrics are truly the feelings I experience when I think of my VSU ... *my* Virginia State University!

"Our hearts beat warm with love for thee, though near or far from thee we be. Virginia State, Virginia State…Hail, Hail, Hail!"

About Jessica Drew

Jessica Drew is a 2011 graduate of Virginia State University. She graduated as a double major student, earning a Bachelor of Science Degree in Accounting and a Bachelor of Science Degree in Management Information Systems. Ms. Drew matriculated through the Virginia State University culture and won the title of Miss Virginia State University 2010-2011. Ms. Drew also joined the Alpha Eta Chapter of Delta Sigma Theta Sorority Incorporated in Spring 2009, and has remained an active member since becoming a member. Ms. Drew's educational background has allowed her to travel across the United States as a contracted auditor for the Federal Government to improve the audit process and remediate findings towards achieving and sustaining a positive audit opinion for the United States. Currently, Jessica resides in Chester, Virginia where she has obtained a permanent career within the Federal Government as a Subject Matter Expert in all matters related to the annual Financial Statement Audit and the remediation of financial audit findings. She uses her knowledge from Virginia State University to ensure her agency can provide reasonable assurance through Financial Statement opinions, in all material respects, in conformity with United States Generally Accepted Accounting Principles and Generally Accepted Government Auditing Standards. Ms. Drew is the Co-Owner of Beyond Décor And More, a full service event planning, coordinating and decoration business, alongside her sister. She was nominated for "top 40 under 40" in the state of Virginia in 2019. Jessica is a world traveler, advocator for all Historically Black Colleges and Universities, and believes without the experiences at Virginia State University, she would not have the drive to succeed through her career and life purposefully.

ALONNA M. GREEN

A Loyal Daughter: True to Orange and Blue

Alonna M. Green

I didn't want to go to college. I was never against it; in fact, I was a fan of college.

Personally, I just wanted to pursue other options. However, I knew college was a non-negotiable for my father, especially because I would be the first generation in my family to attend. So, I decided that if I had to go to college, it would for sure be an HBCU.

Growing up in a melting pot like New York City made me crave an experience that was completely different from what I saw daily. Although my father wanted (more like demanded) me to go to college, he didn't have a preference outside of it being a four-year institution. If it were up to him, I would have attended a State University of New York (SUNY) school. It would have been cost-efficient, and it would have also allowed me to be close to home. However, my stepmother and I were adamant about me leaving New York and taking my talents "down south." So, I set my eyes toward Virginia.

When applying to HBCUs, I wanted to go as far away from New York as possible.

I figured the further I went, the richer the experience would be. I looked at HBCUs in Texas, Georgia and Louisiana. But, for some reason, Virginia stuck out to me. I had family there and it was far enough away from New York. It felt like fate. I did what every college-bound student does. I researched for days on end, trying to gather as much information as possible, until I finally convinced my father to schedule a tour of the school. From that first visit when I pulled up to that lofty hill, I knew there was no other place I wanted to start my journey other than Virginia State University.

I came to Virginia State (affectionately called State) completely green. I expected to make friends, go to class and obtain my degree after four years.

I never, in a million years, could have guessed I would gain that ten times over. Prior to attending State, I was sheltered. Although, I grew up in the big city, I went to private school from the first grade until I graduated high school. When I told my high school guidance counselor that I wanted to attend an HBCU, she told me she didn't think it was a good idea to limit myself to an HBCU. She told me I should be open to other schools that provided diversity. Like I said before, New York is a melting pot, so her take did not shock me at all. I went to school with a myriad of people since kindergarten; however, it wasn't until State that I sat in a classroom where each person in the room looked like *me*. That's when I had my first of many epiphanies.

As I sat there, I realized that my high school guidance counselor couldn't have been more wrong. Black people are not monoliths. Although we look the same, we aren't the same. We all have different experiences, different backgrounds and different stories. Yes, we are all bonded ancestrally. But individually, we have different perspectives and capabilities. I don't think I would have experienced this epiphany at a SUNY school. Virginia State not only molded me, but it changed the trajectory of how I viewed myself and my people.

When I look over my life, I realize that a lot of the decisions I made were made with the wisdom I obtained during my four years at State. At 30 years of age, I've lived in five states. Sometimes, I share this as a fun fact when I meet new people. Every now and then, a person will say something to the effect of, "Wow. I couldn't do that." Usually, I laugh it off, assuming they meant they could never live in the middle of nowhere. However, the last time someone made this comment, I asked them to elaborate.

"I couldn't just up and move somewhere where I didn't know anyone. I would be terrified," the person said.

That's when I realized that, with all of my moves, rarely was I fearful. Some would say I wasn't fearful because of my faith, which does play a huge part. However, some of the best lessons and experiences came from me taking a leap. I took the majority of those leaps in college. You don't go from being a sheltered kid from a big city to living in every region of

America overnight. Virginia State expanded my outlook. It gave me the space to try, even if I failed. It allowed me to use the wisdom acquired from those failures to try again. It challenged me; yet, it provided me with the pieces I needed to become who I am today.

Becoming a Resident Assistant (RA) during my sophomore year helped me with my personal development skills. It also gave me the space to provide important peer-to-peer support to my residents in a plethora of circumstances, such as mental health/self-esteem issues, relationship problems, substance abuse, and academic and financial challenges. Navigating those waters, while juggling my own personal life and academics, taught me the importance of balance. I also had the honor of becoming a member of Delta Sigma Theta Sorority, Inc., which I can say, hands down, was the most impactful decision I could have made.

Making the commitment to be a part of a lifetime sisterhood that is dedicated to the constructive development of its members and to public service, with a primary focus on the black community, was no small feat—nor was it an easy one. That journey I took with 39 other women planted small seeds in me that bloomed over the course of my college career. Those seeds continue to bloom in me today. It acted as a mirror and forced me to not only acknowledge my shortcomings and imperfections, but it also showed me how to embrace them in myself and others. Currently, in my career, I've ran into other people who've attended college and are also a part of sororities and fraternities. There is a difference from those who've attended an HBCU versus those who did not.

HBCU alumni usually mention their school with a sense of pride and vigor. So much so that if their counterpart has never heard of the school, it sparks curiosity. That pride cannot be bought; it can only be experienced. Yes, each of us attended and received our degree from our respective universities; however, some of us experienced lifelong connections. Some of us created legacies. Some of us broke generational curses that existed long before we were even a thought.

The history behind the journey matters. State gave me more than just a few friends and a Bachelor of Arts. It provided me with a priceless experience. It allowed me to experience triumph and defeat. Love and heartbreak. Fulfillment and disappointment. Appeasement and also discomfort. From each of those experiences, I grew and expanded past my own understanding. To say Virginia State molded me into the woman I am today would be an understatement.

It created me into the successful pillar that I am.

Hail! Hail! Hail!

About Alonna M. Green

Hailing from New York, NY, Alonna M. Green attended and graduated from Virginia State University in May 2011 with a B.A in Mass Communications (Radio/Television). While at VSU, Alonna was a devoted Trojan and very proactive on campus. For 3 years, she served as a Resident Assistant. Along with being a Resident Assistant, Alonna was also a part of the Mass Communications Club, VSU Peer Educators, Senior Cabinet Representative, and a member of the Alpha Eta Chapter of Delta Sigma Theta Sorority, Inc. Upon graduation, Alonna relocated to Los Angeles, CA to advance her work in television media. Alonna has worked with The Steve Wilkos Show, The Dr. Phil Show, Judge Alex Court Show, and Deluxe Entertainment Services. Alonna currently resides in Pennsylvania and works for Indeed.

STEVEN HICKS

Family Legacy
Steven Hicks

Most members of my family attended an HBCU. My grandparents, Robert and Dorothy Edmonds, met at Virginia State College for Negroes (now known as Virginia State University) on the steps of Jones Dining Hall.

My grandmother was from Danville, Virginia, the last capital of the Confederacy. She worked several jobs to pay her tuition at Virginia State University, one of them being in laundry. She used to illustrate with her hands how the hot steam made it difficult to handle the sheets, but she persevered. Those times, and others like it, stayed with my grandmother over the years. She leaned on those experiences to teach us life lessons, as was her way. One such lesson that always stuck with me was, "When times get hard, grandson, you get hard with it!" She finished Virginia State University in 1948 and, among many other things, went on to become an educator in Washington, D.C.

Eighty-six miles northeast of Danville is the small town of Kenbridge, Virginia, where my grandfather was born. He grew up on a farm that was purchased and owned by his father, George Washington Edmonds. They raised cows, chickens and numerous crops. He still speaks fondly of the "good old days" when "everybody was poor, so we didn't know we were poor." I think that experience, and many more like it, contributed to the eternal optimist that my grandfather is. He arrived at VSU in 1942 but left after a few semesters to serve in the Navy for the World War II. When he returned to VSU, he completed his degree, graduating in 1949. I recently met one of his college friends. He spoke at length of the days at VSU when they used to sit hotdogs against the windows in the wintertime (to keep them cold) for a meal after their GI money ran out for the month. The overwhelming takeaway was how thankful they were for their experiences at VSU and how thankful they were to have built the relationships they did.

By the time I was ready to go to college, I'd spent most of my life joining my grandparents, parents, aunts and uncles on their trips to VSU for homecoming, visits and other occasions on campus. I enrolled at VSU without taking an official tour of the campus. Having visited as often as I had as a kid, I didn't need one.

The first day I moved in, I met my roommate and the guys in the rooms near mine. I learned that they were from various sections of Washington, D.C. and Virginia. So, we became friends. I picked History as my major because it was a class I enjoyed in high school. I'm sure many of my classmates came to school knowing what they wanted to be when they grew up, but I don't claim to have been one of those people.

Somewhere between those first days and homecoming, my aunt and uncle came to visit for a football game. My uncle asked how I was doing. I don't remember saying anything other than, "Good." But I specifically remember he and my aunt telling me to go see a friend of theirs that served with my uncle at Fort Bragg, Mr. Cortez Dial. He had an office in Virginia Hall, which is the administration building on campus. He warmly welcomed me. After some small talk, he leaned back in his leather rolling chair and said, "If you ever need anything, you come see me." From there, we discussed other topics before I departed. I left his office, feeling like I had a lifeline if I ever needed it. I had an immediate in-road back to something familiar. Family, if you will. I never needed anything from him. But if he reads this, I hope he knows I appreciated him for that. That was just one example, but there were people across the campus who would look out for you. The old folks used to say, "If you see trouble, you go the other way. If you don't, then you'll get beat twice. Once by the person who caught you where you weren't supposed to be, and again by your parents when you got home." That's how VSU was. I never got into anything, but I always knew that I had folks watching to make sure I stayed on the right path. As a parent now, I can appreciate how it must have felt for my folks to know they had eyes on me, just in case.

Freshman year came and went quickly. I went to class, played intramural sports, learned how to be an adult. The great thing about VSU that I probably didn't fully appreciate at the time was that if I wanted to be alone, I had places to go to mind my business. However, if I wanted to be amongst my peers, I could walk outside and find just about anything. From DJs throwing day parties at the student union, to all sorts of fraternal and student organizations holding events, there was plenty to do! There was a family atmosphere of sorts. As I became acclimated to my collegiate surroundings, I took great comfort in knowing that, not just my professors and administrators, but also my fellow students were in this with me. We were all figuring it out together.

My junior year, I met a professor, Dr. Dirk Philipsen. He challenged me to push myself academically. From there, my history degree took a decidedly economic slant. During my last semesters, I spent a lot of time studying the history of our world and considering the economic impact of our past that's brought us to today. At that same time, I got my first real taste of leadership through my membership in and leadership of the Nu Psi Chapter of Omega Psi Phi Fraternity, Inc. I became the Vice Basileus, and later Basileus, of the organization. I also spent some time as a student senator, learning how my classmates ran our campus and contributing to the discussion of how to improve our experience. Those opportunities forced me to develop and, in each of those cases, re-develop my leadership skills. If it wasn't for those formative experiences, I wouldn't be where I am today.

The way things worked out, I didn't stay all four years. I graduated in three and half years. I met a lot of lifelong friends through my HBCU experience. While a handful of them were classmates with me "far above the Appomattox," many of them were from other HBCU's: A&T, Central, Livingstone, Elizabeth City, and many more. I like to think that my grandparents and other family members would be proud of how I played my part in continuing the tradition of developing friendships and contributing to the community.

Mrs. Anita Jackson, the administrator in the History Department, was another such person. Every semester, she made sure I got every class I needed. When it was time to graduate, and I was set to have the exact number of credits I needed for my degree, she made sure I was organized so I would hit all of my targets to finish. I distinctly remember two days before graduation when I was reviewing my records to see if there was an

71

issue with my GPA. Mrs. Jackson sprang into action and helped me. That may seem small, but my paperwork was saying that I was going to graduate "Thank You Laude." I just knew I was supposed to graduate Cum Laude. Somehow, one of my freshman classes had been double counted and was negatively impacting my GPA. Mrs. Jackson told me exactly who to go to in order to get it straightened out so I could get that blue cord for the Cum Laude graduates. She didn't have to do any of that, but she did. As with Mr. Dial, I appreciated that time and energy. It meant a lot to me and I greatly appreciated it.

Armed with these experiences, and my blue cord, I accepted my degree for my efforts and, as my dad would say, I "broke camp." Since that time, two things have been constant for me: my family and change.

One thing I've learned is that the medicine for change is perseverance. I've reinvented myself more than once in the ten plus years since finishing school. I imagine I'll do it a few more times along my journey. Through those changes, my family has always supported me and encouraged me. That family includes the friends I've made along the way. I know I will always have a home at VSU, and I'll always be appreciative of the institution – both of HBCUs at-large and Virginia State University. I'm grateful for all it has done for me and my family. I wouldn't be here without VSU. To that end, my time in school helped me refine my person and my ability to persevere. It helped sustain me in the face of life challenges, large or small. The wisdom I glean from my family, who studied at HBCUs, has emboldened me to maintain the confidence I had as a youngster. I will either find my way or will my way, but I will get there. I believe it was my frat brother, and fellow HBCU graduate, the great Langston Hughes, who wrote, "Life for me ain't been no crystal stair." in the poem *Mother to Son*. In my estimation, we'd all be wise to heed those words.

Hail, State!

About Steven Hicks

Steven G Hicks is a proud graduate of the Virginia State University where he obtained a Bachelor of Arts degree in History with a focus on Economics. During his time far above the Appomattox, Steven was fortunate to pledge the Nu Psi Chapter of Omega Psi Phi Fraternity, Inc. While a student, Steven served as the Vice Basileus and subsequently Basileus of the Nu Psi chapter and additionally held the position of Student Senator in the institutions' Student Government. In his three plus years, he also participated in intramural sports, volunteer outreach in the Petersburg, VA area, and as a mentor to his fellow students. Today, Steven resides in Brooklyn, NY with his wife and daughter and works for an industry leading financial institution covering the Healthcare and Life Sciences industry.

KAYLA BEAL

Branding from the Inside Out

Kayla Beal

Building the perception of my individuality began with my college adventure. It was a maturing process that built the foundation to mold my character. Attending Virginia State University (VSU) was one of the best experiences in my life. When I graduated from Bayside High School, I was looking forward to attending a historical black college or university.

There, the color of my skin no longer mattered; it was about my worth ethic. It was a place where I could celebrate black culture, learn about black history, and experience black love. Being in that environment forced me to evolve spiritually, mentally and physically.

Recognizing my potential during freshman year is where my journey began. Transitioning from high school to college, I was no longer the only black girl in the room. Therefore, I had to go above and beyond to shine in class because we were all equal. There was no excuse to fail. The only person who would hold me back from my dream would have been *me*. Inspired by my godfather, Franz Hall, I set and reached the goal for myself to graduate magna cum laude.

I was raised in Queens, New York, and moving to Virginia was a culture shock. In the neighborhood, everyone was friendly and helpful. People greeted you, even when they didn't know you. At the time, I thought it was extremely weird. I thought to myself, *What is wrong with these people?* In due time, I quickly adopted the culture. I became sociable, friendlier and approachable. These characteristics helped develop my career and build relationships. In the entertainment industry, it's great to be knowledgeable; however, it's more beneficial to build connections. During networking events, I feel confident to smile and start a conversation. Interacting with random people, surprisingly, opened opportunities for me with different networks, such as NBCUniversal, BET, Hulu, Warner Brothers, HBO and much more.

Being away from home was difficult at times. However, it forced me to be independent.

I made a home away from home, where certain friendships grew into family. The people who we surround ourselves with is a direct reflection of our character. At VSU, it was always like a huge family reunion. We all learned, supported, criticized, loved and even hated each other. Nevertheless, there will always be a love there that is unexplainable as a VSU Trojan.

Due to that experience, I can travel for work to different locations and feel comfortable, no matter where I am. The beauty of going to VSU is that we were all from different parts of the world. Ironically, whenever I travel for work, I have at least one friend from VSU who I connect with while visiting a particular city. Whether I am on set for a television show, commercial or movie, no matter the duration of the project, I always feel like I have a piece of home with me.

Balancing life always seems to be challenging. Thanks to my fellow peers, I learned how to play hard and work harder at the same time. Being in an environment where my peers wanted to succeed just as bad as I did really helped me stay focused. I had a blast at the club on a Thursday night, then woke up to early wake-up calls from my friends who made sure I went to class on Friday morning. I didn't know it back then, but I was learning how to balance my life. It's important to stay on course and reach your goals. On the other hand, it's equally meaningful to enjoy life because tomorrow isn't promised. Balancing work, spending quality time with loved ones, spiritual growth and indulging in self-love are all significant. I continue to find new ways to master balancing internally and externally as I self-reflect daily, while encouraging others to do the same.

All my life, I knew I wanted to work in the television and film industry. As I reflect on my childhood memories, I remember watching television and imagining my name in the credits or seeing myself in front of the camera. Now, that imagination is my current reality. This would have been impossible without my connections and experiences from VSU. My major was mass communications with a concentration of Television & Film. After attending classes, meeting with professors and researching, I was still undecided on what avenue to take within my career path.

One day, Professor Dr. Duane Byrge, who was The Hollywood Reporter and Film Critic, said, "Persistence doesn't recognize failure. If you want it, go after it." Although he was teaching the entire class, I felt as though he was talking directly to me. During my junior year, I applied to *The Source Magazine* for an internship. I sent several e-mails and made countless calls, but never got a response. Dr. Byrge's statement screamed loud and clear in my head for days. Finally, I came up with a great idea. I built up enough courage and, with the support of my family, the following week, I went to Wall Street, where *The Source Magazine* building was located.

I stood in the lobby next to the security guard and greeted everyone who came in the building. I ended up meeting the head of public relations.

He asked me, "Why are you in the lobby greeting everyone?"

I said, "I applied here several times and hope to meet the right person to get an interview for a job."

He expressed how impressed he was with my confidence and determination. Next thing I knew, I was in the elevator going upstairs to the main office. I was screaming inside with excitement. They gave me an interview immediately! I gave a presentation that was originally a class assignment and I was hired the same day. I had the opportunity to work with A-list celebrities, such as singers like Monica; rappers like Rick Ross, Wiz Khalifa, J. Cole; and TV hosts like Wendy Williams, to name a few. It was a great experience. I worked extremely hard. I loved the perks of free concerts and radio station visits with Hot 97. Most importantly, I was proud to see my name printed in one of the biggest hip-hop and entertainment magazines.

During college, I yearned to find my purpose and direction for my career. Attending classes, completing assignments and meeting deadlines made me more knowledgeable. However, it was the environment that shaped me into the person I am today. The VSU Church Choir encouraged me to always put God first in all that I do. The Woo Woo Cheerleaders showed me to smile and surround myself with positive energy. The modeling organizations taught me how to walk with confidence. The sororities and fraternities reminded me to form sisterhoods and brotherhoods with my fellow peers. The athletic organizations coached me on the importance of health and fitness. The career-affiliated organizations empowered me to strive for higher goals. Ultimately, this inspired me to run for Vice President of Academic Affairs for the Student Government Association.

Approaching my senior year, I was determined to leave VSU better than the way I found it. I wanted to give more opportunities for my peers. I was passionate about becoming the voice of change that would benefit the students and future Trojans. Being in that role of leadership made me more self-motivated and open-minded. I became a problem-solver. During this process, I studied the significance of branding while campaigning. I learned the importance of building a marketing team, advertising, creating a mission, setting a budget and spreading the word. I developed a catchy slogan: "Seal the Deal with Kayla Beal." That slogan stuck with me for years after college. People would say that slogan to me before they said, "Hello."

Once the officials were elected, we were the liaison between students and administration regarding policies or issues affecting any student. Being in this position prepared me for the real world in my industry. Back then, I was representing the school at different committees. Now, I represent several entertainment companies. Undertaking presentations in front of a boardroom became second nature for me. I used the leadership skills I acquired and applied them in my career of managing a team on set. The skills I learned enhanced my skills as a producer and entrepreneur.

I discovered my career path after I met my mentor, Jesse Vaughan, who is an Emmy Award winning film director and producer. I started working with him on commercials for VSU and immediately became intrigued with his work. He told me stories about his career path, and all the pros and cons of working in the television and film industry. The more stories he shared, and the more projects I helped him with, the more my love grew for the art. It was during that time period where I finally found my passion and direction for my career. I feel extremely blessed that God opened doors for me along the way. Even though it is challenging, I love what I do. I couldn't imagine my life any other way. Every obstacle is unique to each of us, but the demand is the same to push through. Therefore, I encourage everyone to follow your dreams, renew your mind, manifest your goals and never give up.

If I can do it, believe that you can, too.

About Kayla Beal

Kayla Beal is a natural born innovator in today's society. She is a television producer, writer, model and entrepreneur. She was raised in Queens, New York where her parents showed her the importance of education. She excelled her academic goals, earning Bachelor of Arts degree and graduated magna cum laude at Virginia State University. She cultivated a remarkable track record of influencing her peers as Vice President of Academic Affairs.

Beal's career began as a public relation representation for The Source Magazine and BET Networks. Her career flourished as an award-winning producer for NBC Universal, creating content for daytime talk and court shows. In addition, she produced commercials for Tri-Star Studios. She worked with several celebrities such as Jerry Springer, Steve Wilkos, Kimberly Locke, Wendy Williams, Tobias Truvillion, and many more. She is an active member of New York Women in Film and Television, which provides a platform to learn, enlighten and inspire women in the film and television industry.

She is an entrepreneur who runs her own company called "Perception For You, LLC". Providing services of production which include directing, producing, writing, editing, event planning, marketing, hosting, talent consulting and casting. Behind the camera, Beal ultimately enjoys serving at church and participating in charity events.

AMY AGBOTTAH

Culturally Transformed

Amy Agbottah

Virginia State University introduced me to a deeper sense of my culture. My parents are both from Ghana and we spent the majority of my life in Cherry Hill, New Jersey with my two older sisters and two older brothers. I grew up with amazing friends, and I was a field hockey and lacrosse player. However, no one really cared for jollof rice back then. I didn't have many friends who even knew what that was, let alone try it. Let's just say that in high school, my friends didn't look like me. They didn't have hair like me or even had to worry about being a minority. That all changed when I decided to attend college at VSU.

I had an amazing tour guide who convinced me to come to VSU. I was extremely hesitant about being so far from home, but I decided to take a chance and step out of my comfort zone. My freshman year was interesting—a little bit of a culture shock—but I found a way to adjust. VSU seemed so small, but it was big at the same time.

I learned so many things coming to VSU within just a few weeks. I was introduced to "Fried Chicken Wednesdays" in the café, to forums and to teachers who looked like me and wanted to see me grow. This was so different than growing up in Cherry Hill. Though there were so many activities on campus, I was always in the library focusing on my work and trying not to get distracted. It was not until the spring semester of my freshman year when I decided that I could not live in the library forever and that I needed more of social life. Even though I was nervous, I could not continue to miss out on gym jams and social events.

I decided to join the biggest organization on campus: The Betterment of Brothers and Sisters. It was not until I joined the organization that I started to enjoy my college experience. I met some of my closest friends, which transformed my whole experience at VSU. Just when I thought that joining one organization was enough, I wanted to be more involved. During my sophomore year, I decided to not only continue to be social, but to also bring change to the university.

Around the end of my sophomore year, I decided to apply to for the executive secretary position for the Student Government Association. I was lucky to be selected and it opened me up to another side of my university. The SGA opened my eyes to the real college experience—the HBCU experience. It was not until I joined SGA that I went to my first college football game, attended my first homecoming and visited more HBCU's than I could have ever imagined.

Just when I thought that I was done with taking on new roles and joining organizations, I was fortunate enough to pledge the Alpha Epsilon Chapter of Alpha Kappa Alpha Sorority, Inc.

Additionally, I ran a successful campaign for the position of VP of Student Affairs. As the VP of Student Affairs, I was able to implement activity hour and the approval of Greek plots on the university. My desire to impact my university was overpowering.

VSU built my foundation and provided me with so many life lessons. I managed to surround myself with a powerful group of women who pushed me. They have been there to support me in every way. I obtained my bachelor's degree in psychology. After graduating, I received a scholarship to come back and complete my master's degree in biology. I recently completed my master's degree in Health Informatics & Data Analytics from George Washington University.

I am currently living in Richmond, Virginia as a healthcare professional with Anthem Healthkeepers Plus. I plan to grow within my field as I enhance the healthcare world through technology, focusing primarily on changing the world through data analytics and information technology. There is so much that can be done if we simply look at the values of data analytics. With the way the world is constantly changing, telehealth is transforming healthcare as we speak. So many people are going without proper medicine or care because of a failed system or information. Through my work, I plan to change healthcare through technology. This is my technical side, which has served me well. My creative side, however, just sparked.

I have a strong appreciation for details. Growing up, my father poured over research for the littlest thing, like buying a toaster. He would look at every option and feature to make sure he got a good deal on something of high quality. Needless to say, that rubbed off on me. My mother also worked in healthcare, but she owned a catering business part-time. She always brought me along to help with the set-up and even with some of the cooking. As I planned parties of my own for my birthdays, retirement parties, and birthday parties for my parents, I was encouraged to seriously consider pursuing my own business as an event planner. The moment I made that decision, I landed my very first event for a fellow VSU Trojan!

She was planning a birthday party for her mother. What I wasn't expecting was the long nights, rush orders, and the complexity of the completed project. She absolutely loved my work and gave me the validation I needed to know that I was worth the time and the money. Since then, I have coordinated numerous weddings, birthdays, and even proposals under my own wedding and event planning business, Amy Cynthia Events (AC Events).

AC Events is where my love for unique styles and passion for transforming any space into lush, romantic settings has established me as a premier luxury planner for clients all over the East Coast. It has not been easy. There are still times where I really wonder how I am going to find the time to get it all done. That's just it. As a business owner, you just have to *get it done.* If VSU taught me one thing, it's that sometimes, you just have to get it done.

I am so thankful for my HBCU experience and that VSU became my alma mater. The friendships and sisterhood bonds I made at VSU enriched my life. My business has truly grown and changed me for the better. My alumni and personal network always surprise me with the number of referrals I receive from them. If I can say anything about VSU, it is definitely a vibe.

About Amy Agbottah

Amy Agbottah was born and raised in Cherry Hill, NJ. A graduate of The Virginia State University where she obtained her Bachelor's degree in Psychology and Master's degree in Biology. She also went on to earn a Master's degree in Health Informatics & Data Analytics. While at VSU, Amy was fortunate enough to pledge the Alpha Epsilon Chapter of Alpha Kappa Alpha Sorority Inc., as well as hold the positions of VP of Student Affairs. VP of Pys Chi Honors Society and Miss Betterment of Brothers & Sisters. Today, Amy resides in Richmond, VA and works as a healthcare professional, the owner of AC Events and co-owner of Pix R Us Photobooth. AC Events is where her unique style and passion for transforming any space into lush and romantic settings has helped to establish her as a premier luxury planner for clients all over the east coast.

IESHA MONE'E

Always Bet On Yourself

Iesha Mone'e

I never really knew what I wanted to do in life. However, I always knew what kind of woman I wanted to be. I wanted to be successful, well-known and financially free. Looking back at my high school days, I couldn't remember the last time I truly had a straight career path.

I knew I would go to college, but I had no idea where. It wasn't until my junior year that one of my friends I grew up with posted all these photos and cool captions on Facebook. Then, it hit me. I was already cheer captain at my high school. I wanted to learn. But really, I wanted to be social. I applied to five schools—some were Ivy League schools, while others were predominantly white institutions. I ended up getting accepted to all of them, but I chose *thee* Virginia State University (VSU).

Not only was college in the plan, but I got the opportunity to cheer for the best team in the nation. For me, it was a no-brainer. I decided to pack up and take my talents to Petersburg.

I started out as a biology major. After looking at the courses, I decided that wasn't the route I wanted to take. I switched to health and physical education for my major, which, at the time, seemed easy. However, I was in for a ride. I knew I wanted to cheer, but I felt like my career would come later. I had four years, so I wasn't in a rush to figure it all out. Little did I know that I was in for an incredible journey that took hard work, discipline and tenacity.

My first day on campus was check-in day. I met my roommate that day! We also ended up with a corner room, which meant double space. I was so excited. I felt like everything was perfect. In a month, I would move onto campus and everything would be great. On my first day on campus, I stayed out until 3 a.m. *Huge mistake.* That was my first hard lesson on time management. I had to be up by 6 a.m. for freshman week meetings, then hit the gym. Little did I know that three hours of sleep would make me regret staying out so late to socialize.

Things were great my first semester. My GPA was up, and I had nothing to worry about—except Woo Woo cheerleading tryouts. The tryouts were in the spring and were going to be extremely competitive.

I trained hard for three months. I ate everything green in sight, and I practiced any move or chant I knew. When tryouts rolled around, I was one of 100. Before walking in, I almost gave up. Here I was, with the opportunity I'd worked so hard for; yet, I was ready to call it quits.

It seemed impossible; however, in that moment, I learned that you can do anything you set your mind to. I said a quick prayer and decided to go for it. I would have rather failed than to never have tried. I made it to round three. Nervous as ever, I put on my best red lip and rocked my solo piece. During that last performance, I knew I was going to make it. But, so did the thirty girls standing around me. I could barely sleep that night.

The next day, I got dressed in my favorite blazer, a clean white tank and dark denim.

I slid on my Frye boots and walked quickly to check the gym. On that day, I accomplished the biggest goal I ever set in my seventeen years of life. Getting into school wasn't the problem; sticking with it and staying committed to my goal was the *real* challenge. Throughout the process, I met some pretty amazing women. There are fourteen girls who made it with me, and we still talk today. From baby showers, weddings and birthdays, to vacations, business launches and career promotions, we still stick together.

Choosing an HBCU was one of the best decisions I've ever made. I miss the "Fried Chicken Wednesdays" in the cafe. We went there before or after practice to hang out, eat good food, and discuss the latest workload or upcoming event. My HBCU exposed me to traveling, also. Some games were in North Carolina, while others were in New York. I can't believe I performed at Madison Square Garden! Eventually, I joined two organizations: The Student Athletic and Academic Club, as well as The

Future African American Millionaires. Both organizations sharpened my critical-thinking and time-management skills. Sometimes, I had to be at two or three different meetings at one time. Most days, I was running off three or four hours of sleep.

This consistent hustle and bustle created the entrepreneur you see today. When graduation rolled around, I completed most of my classes during the fall semester. I wanted to walk with who I started with, so I took an extra two classes during the spring. In my final semester, I landed a job with Altria. I worked eight hours a day, then attended classes on campus. It was a great deal to juggle, but my HBCU taught me perseverance.

When graduation day approached, I realized how quickly that four years passed by. Here I was, a first-generation HBCU graduate, creating my own path. My parents never made it to college. My older sister decided to start in community college. It felt amazing knowing that I chose my own route and decided to do something that truly made me happy. I went into the education field shortly after leaving Altria, thanks to a friend from my HBCU. From there, my career led me to many industries, ranging from health and finance, to service and telecommunications. My degree got me in the door of most of these positions. My manager or human resources representative would see that I attended Virginia State University and would want to hear all the amazing memories I created.

A few years ago, I was sitting at my desk, working as a personal assistant for one of the top financial advisors in Virginia. I don't know if it was the cold weather, my workload or my crazy schedule, but I decided in that moment that I wanted to be an entrepreneur. I had already earned my license as a nail technician prior to attending Virginia State University. However, I never fully pursued it. That random December day led me to a full salon suite, kicking off Bossy Boulevard Beauty. I thank my HBCU a lot because of the long nights, constant travel and working two part-time jobs while taking 16-18 credits. I was well-equipped for entrepreneurship. Virginia State taught me how to socialize with *anyone*. I was taught to treat the janitor with the same respect as the dean. These small life lessons easily spilled into the work I'm doing today.

Shortly after tackling my salon goal, I developed my clothing line, The Boulevard Brand, a luxury lifestyle apparel line. My line is fashion forward, which was created to bring diversity to the well-known, high-end fashion community. I'm thankful for VSU because I learned to always think outside the box. I learned to never settle. Sometimes, you receive an offer that you can't refuse. But my Woo Woo coach taught me that you don't always take the first offer. "No" always means, "Not yet." I learned from my many days and nights at Virginia State University that you can accomplish anything you put your mind to. Set the bar high. If you fail, pick yourself back up and try again.

The campus in Petersburg is home for me. I always attend homecoming and alumni socials. It reminds me of where I started and how far I have come. Woo Woo taught me many life lessons on sisterhood and the real world. My experience as a member of multiple organizations taught me time management. My entire work ethic was built off the core foundations and principles of Virginia State University. What started out as just an opportunity that I ran across on social media turned into one of the greatest decisions I've made in life.

From setting small goals, like saving money, to paying for my college application fees, creating my dream team, opening businesses and traveling the world, Virginia State University has made me into a proud woman. I am grateful for my experience at my HBCU. The many life lessons I learned during those four years will be with me for the rest of my life.

I live by the quote: "It's not about where you start. It's how you finish. Magic is everywhere, especially inside of you. If you can see it in your head, it can be manifested. Dream big, and never take, 'No' for an answer. 'No' means 'Not yet.' In the right time, the universe will align with everything you desire. If you have to take risks, always bet on yourself."

About Iesha Mone'e

Iesha Mone'e is best known as a serial entrepreneur. The Virginia native has always had the dream of creating a global brand and leaving a legacy. She earned her Bachelor of Science degree from Virginia State University in May 2013. She studied Health and Physical Education which has always piqued her interests. During her four years she was a student athlete performing as a "Woo Woo",member of several on campus organizations, and an advocate for women in business. After graduating she worked in the Health field gaining knowledge in business, finance, and problem solving skills. She quickly realized being an entrepreneur best suited her life goals and began to work on Bossy Boulevard. In 2018 she created the company which consists of The Boulevard Brand a luxury clothing line and Bossy Boulevard Beauty a nail suite. Currently she is working on expanding her clothing line and creating employment opportunities within her company.

TREVON FACEY

Filmmaker

Trevon Facey

Upon arriving at VSU in 2009, I had no idea what to expect for the next four years of my life. What I did know was that it would be life changing. I had a few friends who attended the previous year, as well as my brother, Lyndon Facey. I took on mass communications as my major, with very few skills in the field. Yet, I had a passion to be hands-on and I had the will to create.

My first year was tough. My mother was diagnosed with cancer two months into school, but I kept at it. My concern for her showed in my academic performance. I was ready to leave after receiving a 2.3 GPA at the end of my first year; but things turned around. My mother was given a second chance at life. I looked at it as a second chance for myself, as well. I wanted to bring my GPA up to a 3.0 or better by the time I graduated. It wasn't an easy task.

At the end of the first semester of my sophomore year, I got a 3.4 GPA. It didn't do much for my overall GPA, but it showed me that if I focused, I could make anything happen. I couldn't do it without the support of some key people at VSU. From the financial aid office and mass communications department, to the professors and other staff, they created a commutative experience. At an HBCU, there's a different feeling when you're surrounded by your own people who are on a similar mission. Everyone's goal at an HBCU is to better themselves.

My breakthrough moment that changed the course of my life was the moment I accidently walked into the wrong classroom. That's how I met my soon-to-be mentor and friend, Tim Reid. I wasn't even going to go to my film appreciation class taught by Dr. Burg. I decided to go anyway. As I walked up to the classroom door in Harris Hall, I opened the door and saw that something was different. The dean of our department, Dr. Conway, was introducing a guest speaker. The size of the class was cut in half and my professor was nowhere to be found. Confused, but in a position where I couldn't just walk out, Dr. Conway urged me to have a seat because I was late. So, I did.

An opportunity was being presented to the students in the class to work with an award-winning filmmaker to participate in a filmmaking program. As I listened, it only got better. There was a $1300 stipend for participating and six free credits available in the course as a prerequisite to take part. This was music to my ears. I needed the credit to boost my grades. I needed the money because I was a struggling college student. I applied for the program and this launched my current career as a filmmaker.

Because of this experience, I have been granted the opportunity to travel the world. With my camera and skills I gained at VSU, I am still following my passion in film. I have produced numerous documentaries, worked on two Netflix original films, and filmed content for ESPN's *Undefeated*. Without VSU, none of this would have been possible. I am forever indebted to my VSU!

I love it! I love it! I love it!

About Trevon Facey

Trevon a native of Brooklyn, New York is a Filmmaker and photographer based in Richmond, Virginia. He has been working professionally in video production for over 9 Years. He earned his undergraduate degree in Mass Communication with a focus in film. Facey unearthed his passion for film-making and photography under the mentorship of Actor/Director Tim Reid. Trevon has traveled to Cuba, Trinidad, London, Nigeria, Cape Town, Johannesburg, and Ethiopia, all in the name of film. He has worked on low budget films, documentaries, Netflix Original films even filming for ESPN's Undefeated. Trevon has extensive experience in playing the numerous roles of an independent filmmaker to working with a large crew. Trevon combines his love for travel and filmmaking, telling the stories and sharing the perspectives of people through short documentaries, music videos, and journalistic vignettes.

TARIK K. MCALLISTER

Black Wall Street

Tarik K. McAllister

My fondest moment at Virginia State University (VSU) was graduating on Mother's Day in 2013 and handing my degree over to my mom. We agreed that the bachelor's degree was for her, and any others would adorn my own walls. I never imagined myself going to college.

I associated going to college with debt. I applied to any and every college that had a free application to maximize the likelihood of acceptance, and hopefully, a significant financial aid package. In total, I was accepted to 25 schools. But it wasn't until my grandfather and cousins took a day trip to VSU's spring open house in April of my senior year that going to college even seemed feasible.

I was recently sitting with my daughter and son, Amiya and Omari, when gunshots rang out near our home. It was a sound that I was all too familiar with during my childhood. I didn't expect to hear those sounds in my upper-middle class neighborhood. I recalled how I'd lost multiple close friends to violence, both before and during my college years. From the outside looking in, it seems like I have it all together. Truthfully, I've been trying to figure things out since I was a young boy. All four of the friends I'd lost between 2009 and 2011 had been in my mom's living room. It could have easily been me if I hadn't attended college further away in Virginia.

If I was going to college, I wanted to go to an HBCU. I was all about the black southern experience. I had to experience what I had learned about HBCUs from watching *College Hill* and HBCU homecomings on BET. Media was finally showing black people promoting education and learning, while having fun. I wanted to experience that. I had older friends who had already ventured to Pennsylvania state schools and tapped into the Reserve Officer Training Corps (ROTC) program to help fund their education. At the VSU open house, Captain Miller shared a similar option: four-year scholarship, a stipend, and books—in exchange for eight years of service. I leaned in as grumblings and discomfort filled the space. I was intrigued. I contacted Captain Miller and started the process.

A month or so later, she called to share with me that I was accepted and I received the scholarship. I must have called her another ten times to confirm everything was fine. I couldn't believe it. Through ROTC, I had found a way in, and subsequently—a way out.

I quit my job at McDonald's; I was going to college. I arrived at VSU in August of 2009. I quickly learned that affording tuition, room and board wasn't all I had to figure out. I had a few hundred dollars in my pocket, but I knew I needed some new clothes for the yard. Two hundred dollars goes quickly. There weren't any malls in Petersburg, so I hopped online and ordered a few pairs of Levi's 514s, only to have my card declined when a sophomore was gracious enough to drive me to Walmart for groceries. Ettrick Deli carried me far more days than I'd planned.

I made it to VSU with limited perspective on what I could accomplish in life. My cousin was a social worker. He seemingly enjoyed his job, dressed well, and was one of few individuals I could see myself emulating professionally. According to Google, social workers make $30,000 a year, though. That wasn't really the dream. Spoiler alert: I graduated with a job earning right around that salary. Google also said I could study sociology with a minor in education and do comparable work. Advisors said I couldn't. It wasn't an option at VSU. Captain Miller mentioned many of the ROTC cadets were studying criminal justice, but I realized it just wasn't something my experience as a black man from the inner-city would enjoy. Third time's a charm. I changed my major to interdisciplinary studies with a focus in special education. I was introduced to Mr. Travis, who became a lifelong mentor. He shared that the percentage of black males in the classroom was alarmingly low, and that I was equipped to help fill that gap. It was important that I filled that gap.

In general, life at VSU exposed me to individuals who were willing to think outside the box. I had always been a small fish in a big pond, longing for more than my under-resourced K-12 institutions could afford me. It helped me experience different aspects of black culture. We took different paths but shared a common experience. It was beautiful.

VSU was the nurturing ground for lifelong friendships. I met my son's mother, his godfather, and countless friends within ROTC. My closest college friends continue to be integral parts of my life today. VSU helped me identify my worth and position in society. I appear as a key black male figure in every situation I am in. I was the only black male in my department at Virginia Commonwealth University. Now, as a real estate developer and investor, I'm often working with banks and lenders who see me as black *first*.

I have found that representation and mentorship are both critical to the success of my culture. I've specifically had positive black male role models at each stage in my life, from elementary school to now. I gravitate toward other black men in the real estate industry because it's important that we work together and maintain open lines of communication for ongoing learning. Even in acquiring 40 new units last year, and earning eight figures in assets, our white counterparts are outperforming us by a long shot. My motivation is less about us versus them, and more about the reality that the black community is too far behind in the race of life to compete with one another. I am rooting for people in my circle. I am helping others climb and build. I am creating a life for my family to keep living.

If I didn't learn anything more, I learned that the first-year student who moved into Puryear Hall had far more to offer this earth than he arrived with. I'm paying it forward by hosting and supporting non-profit efforts benefiting youth in the Philadelphia area. I developed the *Ujoma Project* to ensure children are equipped with the tangible resources needed to succeed in the academic space. I'm introducing the world of real estate and development to young people. My team is developing properties for families to enjoy "the hood" and raise children who will shift this earth. When I entered fatherhood, it enabled the desire within me to research ways to create generational wealth and financial freedom for the black community. I've learned to take some calculated risks and always bet on myself.

Attending an HBCU didn't just change my life.

It saved my life.

About Tarik K. McAllister

Tarik McAllister is the founder and CEO of MM Investments & MMI Builders. As an established business owner since 2014, Tarik transforms lives by acquiring, funding, revitalizing and managing distress properties in the Philadelphia and Richmond areas. His other business ventures include Real Estate Investment Consulting, funding, and AirBnB hosting. These strategies have built a multi-million dollar rental portfolio . He is a proud HBCU alumnus, earning a Bachelor of Arts in Interdisciplinary Studies from Virginia State University.

JAMES GOODWIN

The Rippling Effect

James Goodwin

Over the course of ten years, my dream of playing pro baseball moved me thirteen hours away from home, challenged me, frustrated me, grew me and, ultimately, took shape of today's reality—one that I never imagined. In 2010, I was just a kid with a love for the game when I received and accepted an athletic baseball scholarship from the elite Virginia State University (VSU). I proudly, and undoubtedly, became a part of the Trojan family as an established baseball player on a championship winning team. Though VSU offered an excellent academic program, my focus was strictly on their winning sports program, with academics following by a close second. For me, Virginia State University was a new beginning. It became the foundation on which I built my future and created stability with rippling effects.

I was playing my game! This was the life. The culture at VSU shocked this kid from Chicago into meeting and building long-lasting relationships with people from all over the world. Instead of friends, I gained brothers. They made every season one for the books. We learned together and challenged each other to be better ballplayers and better men. As a team, we sharpened each other's characters. Though we conquered many growth spurts together, individually, I grew in self-discipline, self-encouragement and the desire to be nothing short of great. There was fuel behind every hop over those white lines.

It wasn't always fireworks though. There were benches I never thought I'd sit on, and side views I never thought I'd see. Even with the opportunities that came my way, I soon realized that my days as a baseball player would end with my college career after graduation. That was a hard hit. I'd worked my whole life for this, and it was all coming down to what I thought was nothing—at first.

I knew that my love for baseball *had* to outlive that unexpected shelf life. My heart was in it already and I couldn't give up being fully immersed in the sport. That's when the excellent academic program at VSU became more than just about maintaining a GPA in order to stay on the team. It became my life. I took my head off the field and I slammed it into my books. I decided to become more active. To start, I joined the Sport Management "Majors" Club.

Through those development years in the Majors Club, I gained the tools necessary for a career in baseball off the field. After graduating, I did just that. I worked my way into the game of baseball; however, the true test came in finding a way into the game.

The summer after graduation, I accepted an internship with Dugout Media. During my time there, I was a part of the combined staff, where we hosted baseball showcases for youth. We graded their performance on the 20-80 scale, and the best players were chosen to attend an All-American tournament in Indianapolis. The next season, I accepted another internship with USA Baseball as the National Teams Championship Coordinator in Cary, North Carolina, where I also helped other departments to have a smooth, successful season. After that year, I realized that if I wanted to work in baseball, I would have to relocate. In understanding that, I applied for over 50 positions and attended the Baseball Winter Meetings, where all 30 teams prepare for the upcoming year. There, I interviewed with only two teams. I got a call back from The Washington Nationals. They gave me the shot I needed to get in.

I interned with The Nationals for the next two seasons. My first year, I was the minor league video intern for the Hagerstown Suns located in Hagerstown, Maryland. I was fortunate to repeat the internship in the front office the next year as the major league operations intern in Washington, D.C. That year, we made it to the playoffs.

What an experience! When the season was over, I was blessed to be offered a full-time position with The Nationals as the baseball operations video coordinator, where I currently stand. I oversee the video and baseball technology in developing the players who are in The Washington Nationals organization.

In 2019, I was a part of history in my second year in this position with The Nationals in winning the World Series. That accomplishment makes this journey worth every bit! Over the years of grinding in baseball to get to where I am, I owe a part of that to Virginia State University. The years attending VSU molded and prepared me for the fight in life. I thank everyone from VSU who has been on this journey with me. The fight will continue.

I will make Virginia State University proud of this alum.

About James Goodwin

My name is James Goodwin from Chicago,IL. I graduated Virginia State University in 2014 where I was a member on the baseball team all four years and a member of the Sport Management Majors Club. My time at Virginia State has taught me the value of excellence, integrity, and persistence. Since graduating college, I interned with Dugout Media, USA Baseball, and the Washington Nationals. I also became a member of Kappa Alpha Psi Fraternity Incorporated, Richton Park Alumni Chapter. I am currently the Baseball Operations Video Coordinator with the Washington Nationals who are the 2019 World Series Champions. Overall, it may be said that the spirit of excellence, having integrity and being persistent is who I am. Virginia State University, one of the top 10 Historically Black Colleges and Universities in the south instilled in me these values that will lead to continued greatness.

TIFFANY GULLINS

VSU Daze

Tiffany Gullins

Some days, I realize that it's almost insane that my decisions between ages 16 and 18 set the foundation for my entire life. Being that I am from Virginia Beach, I knew for certain that I had zero interest in Norfolk State. At one point, I wasn't even sure that I wanted to go to an HBCU. My great grandfather is a Morehouse alumnus. My grandmother received her bachelor's degree from Howard and her master's degree from Bowie. It took some convincing and a lot of self-searching. I applied to a total of four universities, one that I was not accepted into and two that I was placed on the wait list for. Then, there was Virginia State University.

My best friend suggested that I apply since his older sister, Kandis, was an alumna. I had to call (in true HBCU fashion, wait on hold) to confirm my acceptance. I felt immediate pride the moment I heard, "Welcome to VSU! We will see you in the fall." When I told my family I was going to Virginia State University, I was gifted a copy of Spike Lee's movie, *School Daze*.

I watched that movie 16 times prior to attending freshman orientation. The idea of what I was going to experience was already embedded in my mind. It was going to be an amazing opportunity and I knew every moment was going to be a wild ride. Spike Lee was absolutely right.

I'd never been to Petersburg prior to my first day on campus. I had never heard of it, other than what I saw on BET's *College Hill*. I wanted to keep an open mind, but I can't say I was thrilled. In my mind, I was a big city girl who was getting dropped off in this small town.

I didn't know anyone that well. I knew some kids from my high school, but no one that was a close friend. I convinced myself that I made a mistake. However, I walked into Byrd Hall with an open mind. I couldn't back out now.

My entire family had come to move me in. I lived in the attic of Byrd Hall, all the way at the very top of a building built in 1930. There was no elevator. As I walked up the 94 steps to get to my room, I thought, "I hope my roommate is not here yet, so I can pick my bed in peace."

I walked into room 403 and there she was. Christa hailed from Brooklyn, New York. She didn't even speak to me. She was already irritated by her mom trying to micromanage her unpacking. She was also irritated by the fact that her closet key was mixed up with mine. I looked at my mom and mouthed, "This is going to be bad." However, to this day, she is one of my dearest friends.

We went through some of the best and worst of times in that room that we called "home." Our friendship is one of the greatest things that came out of my freshman year. Actually, I was lucky to make not one, but two really amazing friendships my freshman year. Kiara and I went to high school together, but we were never friends. She used to wear her durag to school. Before she went to class, she went to the bathroom to take it off. She only talked to people she knew, so there was no interaction between us at that time. She just wasn't my type of girl to hang out with. So, when we became the best of friends at VSU, it was a friendship I never expected. Maybe being dropped off in a place unknown to us made us feel obligated to take care of each other. We did everything together. I was beside her when she met her future husband on campus. I was also beside her when she said, "I do." Freshman year at Virginia State University was the true definition of "living in the moment." I chose to major in business marketing at the esteemed Reginal F. Lewis College of Business.

My second year, my sophomore year, was a phenomenal time to be alive. The years 2011 to 2012 were literally defining moments in time. This is when I created the foundation of who I am. That first summer back home after your HBCU freshman year, you come back to your hometown enormously proud. You almost feel like being home is a waste of time. You're just ready to be back with your people! VSU, like many other HBCUs, allows you to bring your car on campus sophomore year. So my

1999 Honda Accord was packed and ready for the ride back down 460 to get me to the Hill.

I adore Virginia State University in the fall, when the air is warm in the morning, hot midday, and cool in the evening. I fell in love with Petersburg. I was a new person in my second year. Kiara became my roommate and we vowed to, this time, balance school and a social life. This was my time to shine. I was no longer a newbie! I had a solid group of friends, my car, a meal plan and Trojan Dollars to spare. Life was so great. I had a confidence that I'd never felt before, and it was such an amazing feeling. This was the first year I became a mentee for new students. To this very day, I continue to mentor. I was also a feature in the Trojan Introduction Program (TIP). My video, "Take Me to VSU" is still on the Trojan Nation YouTube page. My want to have a lifelong relationship with the university was established my sophomore year.

Your support system in college—your village—is everything. They're your family away from home. So what do you do when they all decide not to come back for junior year? I expected one or two of my good friends to decide not to come back to VSU.

Life changes. What I did *not* see coming was literally my entire circle leaving. In the fall of 2012, I decided to come back to Virginia State University, knowing I had no close friends to rely on. But this was a huge moment for me. I was forced to figure it all out. I had to hold myself accountable. I also had to do something that I have the hardest time doing: Making new friends. One thing I had no intention of doing was getting into a relationship. I started dating this guy who used to yell, "Business school shorty!" whenever I'd walk down University Ave. to class. Terrance and I are still together.

One special characteristic of VSU is its social organizations. They are non-Greek organizations that serve different purposes on campus. I was fortunate to become a member of Sista 2 Sista, Inc., the oldest all-female, non-Greek organization on campus. It changed me.

No longer did I need to be the woman who shined brighter than others in a room. I wanted to share my light and shine with others in a way I'd never wanted before. Newfound purpose fueled me to never be afraid to walk alone again. It also let me know that 1,995 women would forever have my back.

I had zero fears going into my senior year at VSU. My advisors prepped me so hard during my junior year that I was ready to apply for jobs. I had three mentees and the real world was about to feel something they'd never felt before. VSU has been credited with having the best business program at an HBCU. I solidified a job in March of 2014. By May, I was graduating with honors from a university that gave me that one chance I needed to change my life. I will always support Virginia State University for giving me so much more than a higher education. This school forced me to grow and evolve over and over, until I was nothing like the girl who started in 2010.

Following my graduation, it was a tough transition from student to alum. I found a healthy way to continue to support VSU and be a full-time adult by joining the VSU Alumni Association, Chesterfield Chapter. In January of 2020, the work I'd been doing as a young alum was recognized when I was awarded a humanitarian award, The Trojan 10 Under 10. I am forever indebted to Virginia State University.

An HBCU experience changes your life in so many unexplainable ways. For the rest of my life, I am a loyal daughter who bleeds orange and blue.

In loving memory of Jordan Greer-Rodgers.

About Tiffany Gullins

My name is Tiffany Gullins, from the great city of Virginia Beach, VA. I came to Virginia State University in the fall of 2010, majoring in Business Marketing at the Reginald F. Lewis School of Business. Through my time at State, I had the opportunity to be very active on campus as a member of Sista 2 Sista Inc., volunteering as a mentor for other business students and with the youth off campus in Petersburg. Virginia State was my second home, and upon graduating in May 2014, I continued to support my alma mater as an active member of both the national and local chapters (Chesterfield) of the VSU Alumni Association. In November 2019, I was selected to receive the Trojan 10 Under 10 Award for my continuous support of Virginia State University through community service, success in my profession, and a lifelong relationship with Virginia State University.

SHAMIR TYNER

Man of Valor
Shamir Tyner

I had to decide to attend a historically black college and university (HBCU) or a predominantly white institution (PWI) nine days before National Signing Day in high school.

As an athlete in my senior year, I received four offers from various universities throughout portions of western Virginia and the state of West Virginia. None of which were HBCUs. I scrambled to decide my future. *Do I head out west, more than seven hours away from home? Would my mother ever be able to see me play a game? How can I be there for my family in case of an emergency?* These questions frequently ran through my head. Frankly, I did not like my responses to any of them. Then, I remembered that all was not lost yet. I had one phone call to make to try to get a scholarship from an HBCU.

I met one of the recruiting coaches from Virginia State University (VSU) at a one-day football camp at a nearby university and took his business card. Seven days before signing day, I contacted him to see if they were interested in offering me an athletic scholarship. He looked at my highlight tape and invited me to the university for an official visit the weekend before signing day. When I turned on campus, I immediately fell in love! I saw people walking on the yard, students studying in front of the bookstore, and sitting, talking, laughing and smiling in front of Foster. Guys were playing basketball at the courts and girls taking pictures in the middle of University Avenue. The Trojan Explosion marching band was practicing in front of Daniel's Gym. I knew I was home. Ultimately, I left with an offer for a full scholarship. The decision was easy, and the rest was history!

Attending VSU helped me realize three things: the importance of networking and building lasting relationships; the beauty of the black culture; and the obligation to be the best "you" you can be in any environment after you graduate. Not only do I believe that I built lasting relationships, but I wholeheartedly believe I have a family at VSU. I met some of my closest friends. I met men that will be groomsmen in my wedding, and women who will forever be like sisters to me. The diversity in ethnicity and experience of the professors made the learning environment practical. It detailed the importance and power of knowledge in the black community. Lastly, I left the university, understanding that my degree can, and does, compete with *any* other degree from *any* other university in the world.

I played football for the first two years of college. I learned quickly that the transition from high school to collegiate athletics is tough and trying. We practiced for hours and we had workouts every day. We had daily film sessions and meetings. I immediately had to adapt to the steep learning curve and start contributing my part to a championship winning team. My first day of training camp, I woke up late for the 5 a.m. conditioning test. I will never forget this day. My defensive line coach chewed me out in front of the team that morning. In the afternoon, he had the conditioning coach work me out until I threw up. I didn't realize it at the time, but the conditioning coach was indoctrinating me into the kind of lifestyle I needed in order to be successful in the world. The team was full of players that faced adversity throughout their lives. Football was a way to destress. We saw a lot of challenges throughout the seasons, but we worked together, as a team, to get through any obstacle in front of us. We grinded, worked hard, sweat together and built up friendships that would stand the test of time.

Outside the field, I struggled academically. The Reginald F. Lewis College of Business is a demanding school. Offering a quality education, the college of business always required professionalism. It became clear that I needed to solicit help from people in my class. The classes weren't large, so the professors knew my name. This is where I began to network. As the years went on, and I declared my major, I had classes with the same individuals. Many of them went on to work for IBM, Deloitte, the CIA and serve as military officers. We helped each other out throughout college. We stayed up late, studying in Gateway, Moore and Ettrick. We created presentations for alumni, the president, major *Fortune 500* companies and stakeholders in the university. We were put into the fire early. With the help of people like Mr. Jonathan Young, Dr. Aurelia Donald and Dr. Adeyemi

Adekoya, I honed my public speaking skills and perfected my negotiation skills. I learned how to wear a suit and how to tie a bow tie while at VSU. I learned how to be a man at VSU.

As at any HBCU, social life was so important at VSU. Every student connected with a social or academic organization on campus. It was beautiful seeing black kids from various experiences and cultures converge in one place and leave smarter, brighter and more skilled than when they arrived. In P.A.N.I.C. 2000, a performing arts organization on campus, I truly found brothers and sisters. Since I've graduated, I've taken trips out of the country, been to baby showers, social events and even funerals with my brother and sisters. VSU brought out skills and talents in individuals and allowed them to be free to practice, perform, and perfect their skills for the community and university. P.A.N.I.C. 2000 provided the student body with a consistent and exciting source of recreation. We put on shows that spoke to relevant cultural issues faced in America. It was a way to express how we felt as educated black men and women.

P.A.N.I.C. forced us to perform at the highest level possible and the organization stressed the importance of networking and putting out the best work possible. With inspiration from members of P.A.N.I.C., I built a videography company that allowed me to make a little extra money while going to school.

Greek life is vitally important to any HBCU. But at VSU, it is a part of the overall experience. Outside of all the parties, every Greek organization made the college experience great. SGA presidents, athletes, professors, staff members, community leaders and musicians were all Greek. All the organizations were special in their own way. But there was one that stood above the rest: Alpha Phi Alpha Fraternity, Incorporated.

The men could dress well. They were smooth and smart. But, more importantly, they were active on and off campus. On Martin Luther King Day, the Alphas organized thousands of students to participate in community service in and around the campus. For move-in day, we helped men and women move their things into their dorm rooms. In February, we actively participated in Black 82, the annual black history production on campus. Alphas were just as professional as they were social. We threw the best parties and the next day, we would go and interact with the elderly at the local convalescent home. We held weekly meetings and decided the future of our legacy on campus. You won't see interactions like these at any other school, except an HBCU.

Today, I serve as an officer in the United States Coast Guard. It would not have been possible to start this career without Virginia State University. It was career day that I met a Coast Guard recruiter. I was intrigued by their scholarship program and decided to sign up to receive additional information. Like any nervous college student, I wrote my name illegibly on the sign-up sheet. The recruiter cared enough to reach out to the university to see if they could help decipher my name. Again, because the university was like a family, it did not take long for the staff members at Career Services to figure out who I was. They not only recognized my name, but they connected the recruiter with me. Had they not taken the extra effort to do this; I would not be in the Coast Guard today.

The Coast Guard has multiple working partnerships with HBCUs, across the country, to diversify their Officer Corps. The value of the men and women at HBCUs is unmatched and big corporations know this! We bring a different level of experience and diversity that cannot be found from other institutions. Through VSU, I understand the importance of waking up early, getting to work before your boss arrives, and leaving after your boss leaves. VSU provided me with all the necessary skills to serve in a leadership capacity. Because of Virginia State University, I am comfortable speaking with high-ranking government officials. I am confident in my skills to get the job done effectively and I am comfortable at relating to people who are facing adversities because I was around it and experienced it at VSU. If I had made the decision to attend a different university, I may have met great friends and received a quality education, but I wouldn't have what I gleaned from VSU. I am uncertain where I would be today without VSU. So many doors have been opened for me, none ever closed, because of my great decision to attend *thee* Virginia State University.

About Shamir Tyner

Shamir Tyner was born in Edenton, NC and raised in Virginia Beach, VA. As a graduate of Virginia State University, Shamir earned a Bachelor's of Science degree in Management Information Systems with a minor in Cyber Security at the Reginald F. Lewis College of Business. In Shamir's senior year in high school, he was blessed to receive a full athletic scholarship from VSU and played on the 2014 CIAA Championship Football Team under Coach Letrell Scott. In 2016, Shamir became a member of P.A.N.I.C. 2000, a performing arts organization, which is where he began monetizing his hobby as a freelance videographer on campus and in the local Petersburg community. During the summer of 2016, Shamir was accepted into the U.S. Coast Guard's College Student Pre-Commissioning Initiative (CSPI) and received a full academic scholarship for his Junior and Senior year. One of Shamir's proudest moments was in the spring of 2018 where he was fortunate enough to pledge the Beta Gamma Chapter of Alpha Phi Alpha Fraternity, Incorporated and serve as a Chapter President. Today, Shamir is an Ensign in the Coast Guard and serves as the Operations Officer and a plank owner, on the U.S. Coast Guard Cutter Robert Ward, a Fast-Response Cutter, based in San Pedro, California. At 23 years old, Shamir is responsible for the safe navigation of a 154-foot ship with a crew size of 24. He is the ship's expert and leader in the briefing, execution, and overall disposition of various missions ranging from Search and Rescue, Counter-Narcotics, National Defense, Alien Migrant Interdiction Operations and more. Shamir has personally orchestrated the response and interdiction of approximately 3,000 kg of pure un-cut cocaine, valued at over 100 million dollars. As the only African-American officer at his unit and only 1 of 3 on the base, Shamir has a personal mission to work hard and ensure he is a voice to those who may not feel comfortable speaking up against injustices. Shamir is able to make a difference in the lives of the people he interacts with, in hopes of better not only the organization but the country.

TAQIYYA HINDS

Dreamer

Taqiyya Hinds

This chapter is dedicated to all the friends turned family from Virginia State University, with a special dedication to my friend and brother, Curtis Bunn. Out of all the great things that VSU gave me, you were by far my favorite. Thank you for your love and friendship. I miss you every day. Keep watching over us, king. #ForeverCurt

This story doesn't begin the way most "How I Found My HBCU" stories begin. I am not a fourth generation HBCU graduate, my parents didn't meet at VSU, there's no legacy chats or college tours for me. My story of how VSU molded me began in my hometown of New London, Connecticut on March 2, 2006. Why do I remember that date so vividly, you may ask? It was the season premiere of BET's *College Hill: Virginia State University*. Yup, that's where this all kicks off. BET got me to VSU!

Up until that point, an HBCU wasn't in my purview. I was hard-pressed on going to my dream school, University of Connecticut. That changed in 2006 when the cast of *College Hill* burst through my television and completely canceled all other options. I was infatuated with seeing young black people who were so serious about their education, all while balancing an extensive social life. Everything about that season and its cast piqued my interest. I hadn't seen anything quite like that until that moment.

In the spring of 2008, I stepped foot on VSU's campus as an incoming freshman.

On arrival, I was completely shocked to see so many hues and variations of black men and women, each displaying a different style and energy. No one person was alike. My God, it was beautiful! I called my friend's mother, out of breath with excitement, telling her, "I have never seen so many black people in one place ever. Wow! I love it here!"

The years to come were riddled with moments of uncertainty. I asked myself, *"Am I doing this right? How long is that validation line? Who picks*

123

an 8 a.m. class? Those late classes sound good until the spring hits and the yard is live. Who's my advisor again? What's their office hours? How packed is the library? If you lived in The Ville, you may have asked, *Do I walk to the cafe? Should I order carry-out? Be mixy in Foster or go to VA's Best?* That wing-ding combo was elite. When you moved off campus, and your cabinets were too bare to make a full meal, those potluck dinners and fellowships saved the day. Man, we really figured it out.

There's a particular cloth that Trojans are cut from. We're an extremely passionate and proud group. From your first class, you are reminded that anything you aspire to be and have is not without hard work, sacrifice and preparation. It is also on that lofty hill where, if you're anything like me, you've built an extensive community that evolved from social gatherings to lifelong bonds. Virginia State University is indeed a special place.

A week after graduation, with no real job prospects, no place to live, a sparse savings account, and my car loaded to the brim, I drove up I-95 North as the happiest, broke college graduate ever. VA, I'm out! I moved back home and lived with my grandparents until I was able to put my next plan in motion: Taking on New York City!

Living in Connecticut meant commuting was inevitable. That was something I tried my damnedest to avoid, but my options were limited and less attractive. So, I commuted six hours round-trip. I know six hours is aggressive, but hey, I had to do what I had to do. A month after being home, I landed a job in finance with a humbling role as the company's receptionist.

My grandparents called it my first "big girl job." Meanwhile, I saw it as my gateway out of their home. For the next ten months, I woke up every day at 4 a.m. I drove twenty minutes to park my car at the Old Saybrook Station where I would take my first train to New Haven. I would then catch another to Grand Central Station in Manhattan—all to be in the office by 8 a.m. After working nine hours, I got off at 5 p.m. and rushed to Grand Central to catch the 5:21 p.m. train home. My adventure landed me at home by 8:30 p.m. I'd talk to my family and go to sleep, prepared to do it all again the next day.

124

Throughout my time commuting, I kept reminding myself of my why. My aspirations to be in New York City was half of the inspiration, but my desires to explore the world of music journalism in one of music's richest cities in the world kept me focused. That was my dream: to write and talk about music. Ten months later, I'm finally here.

I moved into my first apartment in the Bronx. Nothing fancy. It was a small, modest one-bedroom apartment. I rented from a black family who lived upstairs. I was so grateful and proud of myself. After so many sacrifices, I was now preparing for what was ahead. I leaned on my village from VSU and home to get me through it.

I've now been in New York for four years. Since then, I've moved up in the finance world, still not losing sight of my dreams to be in music journalism full time. I started my website, TaqisTake.com, where I've created a platform to review, discuss and engage with others in all things music related, highlighting how music, especially hip-hop, has impacted my life and our culture. I've always considered myself a student in the world of music. Constantly learning and being introduced to the changes in the industry and sounds that we hear daily.

With my curated playlists, social media interaction and artist engagement, I've built a following that has allowed me the opportunity to collaborate with many types of talent, A&R, radio personalities and producers. I've hosted a listening party for up and coming local artists and have continued to grow my brand. In due time, I hope to make TaqisTake one of the biggest household brands in music journalism. Every day, I wake up to battle it out in a city that isn't made for everyone because I know I'm built for it. I couldn't imagine going through those times without the guidance I received at VSU.

So, you ask how my HBCU experience has molded me? It saved me and gave me solace. It added to my already unwavering desire to succeed. I am who I am today because of my HBCU.

It's my forever home.

About Taqiyya Hinds

Taqiyya Hinds graduated from Virginia State University in 2015 with a Bachelor of Science in Criminal Justice and a minor in Mass Communication. Ms. Hinds works as an Operations professional in the Financial Services Industry.

When she is not shaking up Corporate America her multifaceted music platform Taqistake.com has allowed her to express her journalistic creativity with a focus on Hip-Hop culture. She provides readers with album reviews, playlist and original content.

In addition to writing Ms. Hinds is a part-time foodie, adventure junkie, and walking karaoke machine. On any given day Taqiyya can be found exploring the very best of New York City where she currently resides.

HYISHEEM CALIER

The Marathon Continues

Hyisheem Calier

V...S...U! I love it! I love it! I love it! To understand my love for Virginia State University (VSU), you would need to follow the road I traveled to get there. My journey to VSU was paved with failure. Growing up in the projects, as the youngest of six children in a single-parent household, it was a struggle to live in my neighborhood alone. Compared to a kid in the suburbs, I had to grow up faster. I didn't know what it was like to receive an allowance or what it was like to *not* worry about where the money would come from during the holidays. I didn't know what it was like to have my own room. I didn't know that it wasn't normal for your family to come to the neighborhood gym and take you home because there was a shoot-out in your neighborhood. Some days, I didn't know where my next meal was coming from. But I also did not know that, one day, I would go to college.

My journey began as an eighth grader. I was applying to public high schools, like all New York City kids. I was confident that I was going to get into a high school because, not only was I a keen student, but I was committed to my education. But after three grueling months of waiting, I learned that all of the schools I'd applied to rejected me. As a result, I was placed in schools where students failed time and again. Many of them were alternative schools that focused on workforce readiness and G.E.D. prep. These places weren't meant for students hoping to attend college. I was devastated and frightened that my future could turn out similarly.

Feeling cheated out of an opportunity, I questioned, "What have I done wrong to deserve this?" I was left with no answer to a question no child should have to ask themselves: "What did I possibly lack that would make me not worthy of learning?" It didn't take long for me to realize that the answer to my question was simple.

I lacked resources.

Without advocates, without academic preparation for specialized tests, without the money or the means to pay for a private school, I was alone in the fight to figure out my future. This feeling of failure lasted a long time. While one high school accepted me, it happened during the supplemental round and it wasn't a school that was known for its academics. I began freshman year of high school at a public performing arts school, which only accepted me to fill a space. Halfway through the year, my guidance counselor sat me down and dropped what seemed to be a 50-pound book on my desk.

She asked me, "Are you thinking about going to college?"

I responded, "I don't know!"

No one had ever asked me about pursuing education past high school. She showed me the necessary GPA to attend some colleges. At the time, I knew I didn't meet the criteria for acceptance into those universities.

College was just another luxury, and it wasn't meant for *kids like me.* I went to my community center, feeling like maybe I wasn't supposed to succeed in education. I knew that I needed to be in a place where people believed in me. It wasn't until after I spoke with my mentor, Jackie Rousseau, that I could envision myself being successful and could see a clear pathway to higher education. This conversation gave me a renewed focus and energy that pushed me to apply to Rice High School, a catholic school in Harlem with a 99% graduation rate. One of their graduation requirements included gaining acceptance into a college or university. While coming up with a plan for how I could attend this school that seemed so far out of reach, my biggest worry was neither the admissions test nor the application fee. It was wondering how I would pay the tuition if I got in. I passed the admissions exam with flying colors. Still, financial barriers reminded me that not everyone is born with equal opportunity. I knew there were many challenges yet to come.

I wouldn't have survived these moments of feeling unworthy without support systems. No support system runs deeper than family. My oldest sister, Rondrea, has always been the cornerstone of my success. Despite her struggles—such as leaving home at 16 and working long hours to pay her rent on a minimum wage of $5.15 an hour—she has always had my back. If it were not for Rondrea, I would not have been able to attend a school as exceptional as Rice. My sister was the only working member of my family at the time. Although she was struggling to pay her bills, she agreed to pay my high school tuition if I maintained a B-average. After finishing my first semester with an A-average, and making the basketball team, she knew that investing in me and my education was the right decision. More than anything, she believed in me so much that she put herself on the line. This caused me to believe in myself all the more.

Attending Rice High School made a world of difference to me. It taught me about my worth and it introduced me to one of my first mentors, one of the most important male role models in my life, Mr. U. He taught me how to embody all the qualities of a Rice man: responsibility, integrity, courage and empowerment. Looking back on my time at Rice High School, I realize just how important it is to have people who care about you and who are willing to advocate for you. But I wasn't prepared for the challenge that awaited me in the years to come.

As a senior, I was an honors student. I had taken and passed all of my regent exams and advanced placement exams. While I had completed my college application process, I was waiting for my acceptance into college. The April before graduation, my guidance counselor sat me down and explained to me that the colleges I applied to did not receive my applications. Maybe I just wasn't worthy of earning a college education. I felt like my fate was sealed until my other mentor, Barry Ford, saw me crying. He guided me through the Black Common Application. Within weeks of applying, I received my acceptance into VSU. I was going to attend a Historically Black College or University (HBCU), and I overcame that feeling of not being good enough the day I became a Trojan.

Being a Trojan means the world to me. During my time at VSU, I learned how to live on my own and understood the world of disadvantages that people of color are up against within higher education. My life mentor, Dr. Gwendolyn Thornton, showed me the importance of higher education through the world of social work. She also introduced me to Radford University, where I received my master's degree a year after graduating from VSU. While at VSU, I had the honor of serving as vice president and president of Student Government, and a Board of Visitors representative. In these capacities, my love for VSU grew tremendously. Five thousand students trusted me to represent them, which let me know that my leadership was appreciated. I even had a staff of ten and a working budget.

During my summers at VSU, I was inspired to help my community back home. Every summer, I came home with a mission to learn more about how I could advocate for my neighborhood. Advocacy led me to intern for both New York City Councilmember, Corey Johnson (now also Assembly Speaker) and then Newark Mayor, Cory Booker (now Senator). Working for public policymakers helped me understand grassroots politics and led me to a social work internship with youth at the Virginia Department of Social Services.

As a budding attorney, I often recognize that I would not be where I am today if it were not for the loving support and care from individuals along this journey. They were there to get me through the moments where I could not see the forest for the trees, let alone my future. Furthermore, the love I have for my HBCU is deep because I remember the experiences I have overcome—both to get there and while navigating higher education. VSU showed me that when I became a Trojan, I joined a family of individuals who will follow me throughout life. So, every homecoming season when I return home to VSU, I am reminded of just how much I love it, I love it, I love it!

About Hyisheem Calier

Hyisheem Shabazz Calier is a multi-faceted creative, hailing from the combined housing projects of Elliott Chelsea, located in New York City. He is the founder of H.O.O.D. Brothers LLC., an entertainment label and lifestyle brand consisting of the acronym "Hustle Out Of Desperation." During his undergraduate years at The Virginia State University, Hyisheem began to tap into his creative passion by producing the university's theme song. His interest in music ultimately resulted in the release of his first iTunes single "Radio". Calier's outgoing personality combined with his leadership and advocacy skills led him to becoming the University's Student Government Association President. Calier's talent and drive was recognized by HBO, making him a main feature in their award-winning documentary, Class Divide. As a first-generation college student Hyisheem Also became the first of his family to graduate from college, obtain a master's degree in social work and also pursue a law degree.

JHADEE GORDON

Coming to America

Jhadee Gordon

I was the first person in my family to live and attend school in America. When I had to decide what college to attend, I truly had to make the best decision—not just for myself, but for the generations that would come after me. Born and raised in a little village on the west bank of Guyana, I migrated to the United States at 14 years old. While in high school, I didn't know what I wanted to major in when I got to college, let alone what an HBCU was and if I wanted to attend one. As senior year approached, I was blessed to have a black woman as my new counselor. She was not an HBCU grad, but she educated me on the options of attending an HBCU.

My mother wanted to keep me in the state of Virginia, so we settled on applying to my dream school at the time, Stony Brook. We also applied to three other nearby colleges: Virginia State University (VSU), Norfolk State and Howard University. I wasn't accepted into Stony Brook. However, I was accepted into another school in New York, Howard and VSU.

I scheduled my visit to Howard because I heard so many great things about the university. Upon arrival to Howard's financial aid office, my friend's mother gave me the rundown. She told me that VSU would be the best financial decision for me.

So, I applied, got in, and was dead set on finishing my freshman year at VSU so I could transfer to Howard. Once I got to campus on move-in day, I was so pleased to find out that the single room I was appointed was *massive*. That was a plus because, being an only child, and also the first person to go off to college in the U.S., my mom was worried about me. But I was blessed enough to have a single room my first year. However, living in the single room comes with more expenses.

My balance was due, and I had no idea how to get money for school. Coming from Guyana and being the first to go to school, loans are taboo. But we took a chance and took out a loan. At the end of my freshman year, because I kept my grades up, I was awarded a university scholarship, which covered a chunk of my academic career at Virginia State University. Financially, things got better, and I decided to stay at VSU. That year, my stepbrother had graduated college, which allowed me to use the tuition reimbursement program at my stepfather's job. Financially, I was truly blessed.

So, with all the financial things taken care of, I still had to decide whether or not to stay at VSU. The economics program at that time was going through a rocky accreditation, and no one was able to help me with my schedule. I wanted to keep my major, but I didn't want to leave VSU. I had made some lifelong friends and supporters, and I didn't want to restart. I decided to change my major. I went from an economics major with a minor in accounting and finance to an accounting and finance major.

Virginia State University pushed me out of my comfort zone. When I moved to America, I didn't know what my life was going to be like. Everything at home was working out so well. Having to start over really took a toll on me. When I got to VSU, I realized that this was my new beginning. In high school, I didn't come out of my shell much. But at VSU, I took the world by storm. Even in my timidity, I ran for freshman class president. When I didn't come out victoriously, the current president saw something in me and reached out for me to still be a part of the board. The experience and the friendships I gained from being on the freshman class council propelled me for the rest of my time at VSU. My sophomore year, I was sophomore class president.

I joined the National Association of Black Accountants and I kept a 3.5 GPA.

As the years went on, I used the skills that I learned in my leadership roles to help me secure internships, scholarships and, in 2017, a full-time job. I served as the junior class president and the resident hall president of More Hall. I was also fully involved in networking events presented by the Reginald F. Lewis College of Business. Once senior year rolled around, I was ready to take on the world. I was now on the royal court as Miss Virginia State University, second runner-up and served as the secretary of the National Association of Black Accountants. I was recognized as senior of the year by the Honors Program and was vice president of The Caribbean Students Association. All the while, I managed to keep my grades high. I also secured a job with the Grants and Contracts Department, which helped me understand accounting on a different level.

All in all, VSU transformed me into a well-rounded individual. I hold Virginia State University near and dear to my heart, and I effortlessly advocate for those students and for the betterment of the university as a whole. Without VSU, I truly don't know where I would be today. I don't think I would have the job that I have, be the person that I am, or know the people who I know if God didn't place me at VSU.

About Jhadee Gordon

Jhadee K. Gordon is a Guyanese born American currently living in Atlanta, Georgia. Jhadee is the daughter of Eve Patrick and Ken Gordon. At the tender age of 14 she migrated to the United States to live with her mother and reap the benefits of the land of milk and honey.

Throughout her 10 years living in America she has accomplished a wide range of achievements. In high school she secured her place on the honor roll all four years. She graduated in the top 30 of her high school class and secured a $30,000 scholarship to attend a college in upstate New York. As she is the first to migrate and attend school in the United States, she carefully weighed her options and decided to pursue higher education in Virginia. Jhadee attended The Virginia State University where she gained a Presidential Scholarship after her first year of attendance. During her time in college she was the sergeant-at-arms for the freshman class, sophomore and junior class president, and received the outstanding junior and outstanding senior awards. While in college she participated in the Miss Virginia State University pageant where she was crowned Miss Virginia State University 2nd runner up. She's also served as the residents' hall president (2015-2016), the Vice President of the Caribbean Students Association (2015-2017), Secretary of the National Association of Black Accountants (2016-2017) and a mentor for first year students with the Trojan Leadership program. Jhadee graduated in May 2017 with a Bachelors' degree in Accounting and Finance.

Jhadee currently works for a global accounting firm in Atlanta, Georgia. She is an associate auditor with plans of opening her own financial literacy firm in a few months to educate people, specifically those in the black diaspora, how to master their money, help women-owned and black owned businesses develop financial plans and budgets and travel the country teaching HBCU students about all things finances. She was among the inaugural class of recipients of the Trojan 10 under 10 award; an award given to alumni of Virginia State University who have continued to pour into the university even after they have left. Today, Jhadee has brought it full circle by competing in the Miss World Guyana Pageant and returning to her home.

JOY HICKMAN

Perfect Pond

Joy Hickman

Decisions. I have found myself reflecting on many decisions lately! I have been truly at war with this word. What does it mean? Is it me making the hundreds of decisions daily, or are they actually made for me? I like to believe that every choice is mine to make, and that the one I make is the *right* one for my journey. My background has impacted all of my decisions, and I am so thankful for the people around me who have made decisions on my behalf, which have put me in positions I never dreamed I would be in. Out of all my decisions, one of the most profound was the one that landed me high above the Appomattox at Virginia State University (VSU).

I had to make my first big choice in late July of 2013 when I chose to sign my first contract and play basketball for VSU! Virginia State University was truly the best decision I could have made for so many reasons. Before I tell you why, allow me to tell you what led to this moment!

Growing up, I always told myself I would never do certain things! It's a rather negative outlook on life; but in my mind, knowing exactly what I did *not want* was the easiest way to make a decision. So when it came time to start thinking about what I would do after high school, I knew three things:

I would not be someone who would get a job straight out of high school.

I would not attend an all-girl college.

And I would not attend an HBCU.

I had an incorrect, negative stigma toward all these things! I couldn't have been more wrong! When senior year rolled around, I didn't have the offers on the table that I thought I would have. I got really anxious because I knew what I did *not* want to do. More and more each day, it seemed that one of the three things I *did not want* to have would become a reality! When I finally chose VSU, it was originally because I thought I was picking the lesser of two evils. I was skeptical, but I chose VSU based on a few conditions.

First, school had to be free. I had to be playing basketball, at least. And, if I hated it, I would come home and figure out what was next. After my visit in July, I changed my mindset to accept whatever my next step would be. I decided to make the most out of it. I signed my letter of intent and, once I arrived on campus, my eyes were opened to a culture I wasn't close to. I was exposed to backgrounds I wasn't aware of, and extremely intriguing, intellectual, inspirational people—from the leadership to the student body, and even the community. I warmed up quickly and started crushing my schoolwork, social life and basketball!

VSU was the perfect pond for me to learn how to swim. It was the perfect transition to the "real world!" VSU gave me the safe environment to be multifaceted. At VSU, I always chose to go to class and to put in the work to maintain a good GPA. I attended every social event I knew about, and I was involved in every organization that would accept me as a leader, member or consistent supporter. My decision to go to VSU—and my decisions while at VSU—created an incredible experience that I wish everyone could experience.

When you are young, you don't understand the importance of being surrounded by people who invest into you. You don't truly value those who are genuinely rooting for you. I know now that so many people helped set the stage for me making some of my biggest decisions. From the time I was born, I was always immersed in this loving atmosphere that provided nutrients for me to grow, discipline and the ability to know when a second chance is beneficial. I grew up in a two-parent home with six siblings, five of them being older than me. They paved many different ways for me to find success. I had examples of successes that came easy and ones that didn't come easy, but they all came in the perfect time. What I didn't know is that this is what I was looking for in college.

VSU was my match made in heaven and so much more. I would not have graduated top of the College of Engineering and Technology without the help of professors who were strict with deadlines, extremely challenging with academics and accountability, and had high expectations for our quality of work. Our professors also had enough heart to make exceptions for me, allowing me to take tests early so I could play basketball and receive an engineering degree at the same time.

I would not have had such a successful basketball career if it weren't for Coach Hill, Coach Millz and Coach Penny. They were the perfect mixture of strict timeliness and dress code, rigorous athletics, with high expectations for winning and losing with poise. I would not have been finally convinced to truly be the change if it weren't for President Abdullah being strict with enforcing the university rules to faculty, staff and students alike. The staff was supportive of all things that were important to me, and they always had an open door to listen. These are just a few employees of VSU who I encountered who made sure my experience was "one for the books."

While every school may have people like this, VSU had people whom I met freshman year who added to my confirmation that I made the right choice. A VSU alum used to ride his bike through campus every day for his workout. I came to befriend him because he loved VSU. He attended all the football and basketball games. I used to love the two-minute conversations we shared when I brought him water after he reached the top of the hill. The Billups were another confirmation that I chose the right university. They were such big VSU sports fans and they were my favorite boosters! They are the reason I am passionate about continuing to improve VSU sports! When they gave me the tour of the new multipurpose center, I went nuts. VSU is all about building relationships with people, and my experience is proof that VSU produces impactful people who make decisions to change the world they live in.

I am Joy Hickman, a proud, first-generation HBCU graduate and an extreme advocate of VSU! VSU has so many versions of success to offer. Whether you are there for two years or twenty years, I promise you that it won't let you leave empty-handed. Without VSU, I am sure that I would not be where I am today. I left school debt-free with a degree; I work at Deloitte, and I live in a condo in Atlanta that I bought within two years of working.

Most importantly, I started a scholarship at the school I love so dearly and I always will. I am so glad I went to VSU!

About Joy Hickman

Joy Hickman was born and raised in the first state, Delaware. She is one of seven children and credits who she is to her family, sports, and most importantly choosing to attend the Virginia State University! Although she believe VSU chose her, she credits VSU to being the final component of "her total package". Growing up she never had to worry! Her parents and older siblings took on the burden which allowed her to shape her goals to be able to pay it backwards and forward. When your biggest worry in life is how to be your best you, it's amazing how someone can grow! Joy chose to dedicate her adolescent life to athletics and academics and she never backed down from a physical or intelligence challenge. If you ask her to this day if she has ever lost before, she will tell you "I have never lost anything before I just ran out of time." Growing up an athlete, Joy has been successful in volleyball, softball, competitive cheerleading, and eventually decided to take her talents in basketball to VSU. While at Virginia State University Joy was a CIAA Champion, member of student senate, Chairman of events for NsBE, Mrs. Langston, VP and President of SAAC, and so much more. Not only did she take leadership in organizations, she developed relationships with VSU as a whole. From the cafeteria staff to the security staff, professors to the President, Joy Hickman was a well known name to many on campus. Joy feel in love with her HBCU and always enjoyed giving back. She was always willing to help where needed and give without being noticed. Since graduating Joy has begun her career with Deloitte and started her scholarship fund at Virginia State University and continues in her forward thinking of "what's next".

There's No Place Like Home

N'Dea Jackson

As cliché as it may sound, from the time I stepped foot onto Virginia State University's campus, I knew I was home. From as early as I can remember, when I thought about college, I knew I wanted to attend an HBCU. As the daughter and eldest child of a *proud* Howard University alum, I was convinced from birth that Howard would be that HBCU. When I got the opportunity to tour HBCUs in April of 2013, I went into the experience completely open-minded. I gave every institution an opportunity to sell itself. Being that the majority of HBCUs are southern schools, and I am from Boston, my only major request was that the university that I chose made me feel at home.

After a 24-hour bus ride from Boston to Tallahassee, my HBCU experience began. As we drove the east coast and toured HBCU after HBCU, I deciphered the things I liked and disliked about each institution. Did they have the program I was interested in? What did students who we met on the tour have to say about their experiences? How big was the student population? Most importantly, did my initial contact with the university feel like home? While a few of the universities checked off multiple boxes, none of them gave me the overall experience that VSU did. They had my program of choice. The student ambassadors on my tour were so welcoming. They had nothing but positive things to say about their HBCU. Even the things that they wished were different, they still made them sound like positives. VSU's student population and campus size were the perfect size for me since I'd come from a graduating class of 250 students. Most of all, 576 miles away from my place of residence, I felt like Virginia State University was a place that I could call my home for the next four years.

Upon my return home from the college tour, my parents and I sat down and discussed my opinions on all the schools I had toured. When I told them that VSU was the school for me, we had a long conversation about why. Then, we planned a trip to Virginia so they could see the school for themselves. We missed our scheduled tour time due to the traffic, but the admissions staff was very understanding and gave us a personal tour. The level of attention and care that my family and I received on this tour was unmatched. We set the precedent for the encounters I had during the four years I spent there. By the end of the tour, my parents were sold. Everything about VSU seemed too good to be true! After completing my SAT attempts, and submitting my application to the university, I received my acceptance letter and a full, four-year academic scholarship!

I remember the day that we drove up that front hill to begin my freshman year at VSU. With my car packed to the brim, and everyone overcome with emotions, I was finally beginning what would be four of the best years of my life. After multiple trips to my room on the second floor of Langston Hall, and a trip to Walmart, it was finally time for my family and I to part.

I was both nervous and excited. I was starting a new journey in a brand-new place, all alone.

As the oldest of three, I have always been responsible for setting the example. This was, by far, the biggest example that I would have to set. Yet, through all the emotions that I was feeling, I trusted God. I truly felt like this was where I was destined to be. I don't know if I have ever been more correct in any other decision.

The foundation of everything positive about my college experience stems from my days in Langston Hall and my time as a Trojan Introduction Program Leader. Living in Langston, I was able to meet some of the most amazing individuals, who would grow from college friends into forever family. I will never forget the late nights studying together in the basement, sharing cabs, or all piling into Cody's Oldsmobile to go get food off campus. I won't forget the manhunt games behind Virginia Hall and shuttle trips to the mall family outings. Everything about this time in our lives was so simple, yet so riveting. In the second semester of my freshman year, I attended an informational meeting for the Trojan Introduction Program, VSU's orientation leaders. I was apprehensive at first because I realized that being selected would mean that I would spend my first summer as a college student away from my family. But when I thought back on how much fun I had at my Trojan Introduction Program session as an incoming freshman, I knew I wanted to provide that same experience for incoming students.

Although the program was geared toward helping incoming students prepare to enter their freshman year of college, I gained a great deal from it, as well. We bonded with each other and made great connections with faculty and staff who were on campus throughout the summer. By the time the school year started, and before we even realized it, I had gained a whole new support system. This is exactly what the HBCU experience should be about. It is safe to say that my freshman year, and the summer following, I was one of the happiest, broke college students. I went on to be a coordinator over the program for the following two academic school years.

That leadership experience set me up for future leadership experiences, such as being vice president of the Student Government Association for the 2016-2018 academic school years. This position helped me find a voice that I didn't even know I possessed. VSU didn't give me a voice; rather, it helped me unleash what was already within me. I used this position to institute changes on campus, such as mandating the singing of the Negro National Anthem at all university events. I also instituted change on a global level. In May of 2017, I had the privilege of participating in a three-week long study abroad trip to the impoverished village of Skoura, Morocco. Upon my return, I organized a school supply drive and collected over 3,000 school supplies to send to the students at the schools in the village. The culmination of all of these leadership experiences led me to one of my most valued accomplishments: joining the only sorority, Delta Sigma Theta Sorority, Inc. These priceless opportunities are some of the many ways in which my HBCU challenged me to be better in all ways, at every turn.

While academics are the main reason that we enroll in college, the HBCU experience is about so much more. Being a student at an HBCU was so empowering because I was able to learn from and establish connections with black professionals in the field that I aspired to enter. Through alumni connections and partnerships, I landed a full-time role at IBM as a technical solution specialist. In these turbulent times that we are currently experiencing surrounding COVID-19, I am also leading an effort sponsored by HBCU alumni from my company to bridge the gap for displaced students in need by providing them with laptops so that they may continue their studies this semester. I constantly reach back to make sure that those same opportunities are afforded to the next generation of Trojans, the same way it was done for me.

When you graduate high school, many people tell you that your college years are going to be over before you know it. That statement didn't hit me hard until May of 2018 when it was time for my new family and I to part ways. Looking back on my years at VSU, I never became overwhelmed with homesickness the way I initially anticipated. I definitely always missed my family and friends from home. But because I selected a school that felt like home, I was able to extend my family farther than I ever thought possible. I am happy that I took advantage of every opportunity that I could at VSU. From the Honors Program and studying abroad, to pledging the Alpha Eta Chapter of Delta Sigma Theta Sorority, Inc., I *lived* my college years. I would not be who I am, or where I am, without my experience at Virginia State University.

I was a young, black girl from Boston, who arrived in Petersburg, Virginia in 2014 in hopes of blazing a path of my own. No family. No friends. Just faith. VSU has made me a better friend, mentor, student, sister and overall person. I have been more than prepared for every adversity that has come my way. My HBCU education has landed me a spot in the Master of Data Science program at Syracuse University, where I will graduate in 2021. No matter where my walk in life takes me, I am thankful to always have VSU to call my home.

Hail, State!

About N'Dea Jackson

N'Dea B. Jackson, born and raised in Boston, MA, graduated summa cum laude from Virginia State University in May 2018 with a Bachelor of Science degree in Computer Engineering and a minor in Mathematics. While completing her undergraduate studies at VSU, N'Dea was an active force in her campus community, involved in various academic, volunteer, and social organizations including: The National Society of Black Engineers, Kappa Mu Epsilon Mathematics Honors Society, study abroad, as well as both the Trojan Introduction and Trojan Leadership Programs. She served her university in positions such as Student Government Association Vice President of Academic Affairs (2016-2018) and was a Presidential STEM Scholar in the Honors Program. N'Dea was also initiated as a member of the Alpha Eta chapter of Delta Sigma Theta Sorority, Inc.

Upon graduating, N'Dea accepted a full-time offer with IBM as a Technical Solution Specialist in the Summit Program. Through this position, N'Dea continues to give back to her beloved Alma Mater by aiding students in securing internships and full-time offers, preparing the next generation for greatness.

CODY E. MITCHELL

Growth Zone

Cody E. Mitchell

The illustrious Virginia State University (VSU) is a school of rich values that has a focus on diversity, engagement, excellence and its student population. It's a place of higher education that stands on the foundation of over one hundred years of American history. Most importantly, this HBCU has changed the lives of many and will continue for lifetimes to come. The difference between HBCUs—especially VSU—and all other schools of higher education is very distinct. My alma mater has given me an experience that I couldn't have found anywhere else. From the people I have met and the things I have experienced, to the traits that have built me personally and professionally, VSU is a place where all may go and drink from the fountain of knowledge.

I first discovered HBCUs when I was a senior in high school. My ultimate career goal was to become a commissioned officer in the United States Coast Guard. I applied to attend the United States Coast Guard Academy and was unsuccessful. However, I did not give up on my dreams. I tried to enter the Coast Guard through the College Student Pre-Commissioning Initiative (CSPI). This is a scholarship program designed for students attending minority institutions to diversify Coast Guard officers. Upon graduation, CSPI students attend Officer Candidate School and receive their commission in the Coast Guard.

I found VSU's website through CSPI and was extremely impressed with the degree programs, notable alumni and on-campus activities. The day I took my campus tour, my family and I immediately felt the hospitality, family atmosphere and unlimited opportunities. When we were driving back home that night, I knew VSU was the only university I wanted to attend. It was the only university I applied to. I owed much thanks to my first mentors on campus, Mr. Neal and Ms. Burwell. It was because of them that my initial experience at an HBCU was so memorable, which led me to ultimately choosing this great university.

My freshman year, at first, was very uncomfortable. I did not initially feel like myself, nor did I feel like I could express how I felt. People constantly asked me, "Why are you going to college here?" I was born and raised in a predominantly white community in Eastern Pennsylvania. For the first time in my life, I was in an environment where I was the minority in my classes, and even in my way of thinking. I felt like I couldn't speak freely on certain topics because of the judgement of others and how it may affect me outside of the classroom. As my HBCU career progressed, this drastically changed for the better to allow me to grow as a member of society.

My second semester during freshman year, I was introduced to a group of young men and women who are now family. They will always be my closest friends. We all lived in Langston Hall, which, at the time, was the residence hall for all of the students in the honors program. We socialized and studied together. Throughout all four years, we continued to grow together and pushed each other to become better than we were the day before. We always have each other's backs—no matter if the person was right or wrong. Once our student days were completed on the great campus of VSU, we all stayed in touch and we see each other quite frequently. We still bounce ideas off each other and we tell each other the truth, no matter how challenging it may seem. It's a connection that cannot be explained, but can only be found at an HBCU.

I studied criminal justice and sociology during my time at VSU, and my way of thinking became more diversified. While my department had so many great professors with so much wisdom, I have to thank Dr. Zoe Spencer and Dr. Nishaun Battle for pushing me and never letting up on me. The information they exposed me to expanded my way of thinking. I was now in an environment where the topics of conversation were on white privilege, the school-to-prison pipeline, social institutions of one group and how it affects social groups of another, important black history that tends to get lost throughout generations, social injustices and so much more. Before, it was people who looked like me trying discuss topics like crime rates in other societies and believing possible stereotypes that we might have heard growing up. In reality, we had no knowledge or basis in fact of what was truly going on in the world.

At VSU, I heard other opinions and people's process of thoughts and feelings from places far from my own. I was able to dive into theories, such as Critical Race Theory, and got to the base of issues to determine the truth and what was truly occurring. I had tough conversations on things I, at one point, didn't even know existed. This information would have never come to me if I did not step out of what I knew growing up and placed myself in a place that was not always comfortable, yet allowed me to grow.

While I may not agree with every belief or topic from the people who I connected with at VSU, I can stand on the other side, hear where that person is coming from and meet somewhere in the middle. VSU has given me these traits. I constantly use these traits in my world of work in the military, working with people of all backgrounds from all over the world.

My sophomore year of college, I became a member of the Virginia State University Chapter, the Alpha Phi (E) of Kappa Alpha Psi Fraternity, Inc. This was an experience I will never forget. It gave me brothers who will forever be by my side, along with endless opportunities and a wide range of networking connections. I knew Greek life was a thing at college, but I never knew of The Divine Nine organizations until I arrived on campus. These organizations were composed of leaders on and off campus, people who were always making lasting impacts to the university and the surrounding community.

As I developed mentors on campus, such as Mike Jones, Danny Giles and Xavier Richardson, I also discovered that they were members of this noble group of men. I continued to develop myself by serving in numerous leadership roles, such as Polemarch (also known as the president) of my chapter and Region III Board Member of the Eastern Province. Throughout these special experiences and guidance at VSU, Kappa Alpha Psi Fraternity, Inc. continually invested in my future, never steering me in the wrong direction. These men that I surrounded myself with cannot be found anywhere. This is a special group of men dedicated to achievement and training leadership to up and coming generations. While I joined Kappa

155

Alpha Psi Fraternity, Inc., all Divine Nine organizations are invested in helping their communities and provide great resources to others. I am honored to be exposed to these types of organizations that I once never knew existed.

While I attribute much of my success in life to God and family, I would be remiss if I didn't also give much thanks and appreciation to Virginia State University. I will never be able to fully comprehend the growth and development I have gained throughout those four years. There is so much to talk about—from campus ministries with Reverend Douglas and Ms. MC, to community service opportunities. Today, I proudly stand as an HBCU graduate from Virginia State University.

My initial goal at VSU was to join the United States Coast Guard as a commissioned officer. I write to you today with that goal achieved and so much more.

I once thought I would go to class and go back to my residence hall and join the Coast Guard, but God and VSU had a bigger, deeper plan for me. People often say, "There is no comfort in the growth zone and no growth in the comfort zone." That's what my HBCU experience fostered in me. From my leadership positions serving as Langston Hall president my freshman year, to student body president my senior year or my study abroad in Cuba, VSU allowed me to mature and flourish in whatever opportunity or challenge I encountered. My HBCU experience diversified my way of thinking, gave me countless mentors who continue to invest in me and friends that I will always consider family. These are experiences that you will not find anywhere else but VSU.

If you are a graduate of an HBCU, make sure you give back to your respected alumni association so others can have a memorable experience just like you did. If you are considering going to college, and you're not sure if you want to go to an HBCU or not, take that chance.

I promise you won't regret it. You will have the time of your life and gain memories you will cherish forever. Virginia State University will forever be Virginia's opportunity university.

About Cody E. Mitchell

Cody E. Mitchell is a native from Douglassville, Pennsylvania and is the son of Brian and Stefani Mitchell. Mr. Mitchell graduated from Virginia State University, VSU, in 2018 summa cum laude with a B.A. in Sociology and a B.S. in Criminal Justice. During his time at Virginia State University, he proudly served as the Student Government Association President and Student Representative on the VSU Board of Visitors, 2017-2018. Mr. Mitchell has shown pure dedication to his alma matar and was awarded the Trojan 10 Under 10 Award in 2020. Mr. Mitchell is a lifetime member of Kappa Alpha Psi Fraternity Inc. and proudly holds the honor as the 93rd Guy L. Grant and the 45th Byron K. Armstrong Awardee. Mr. Mitchell commissioned as an officer in 2018 in the United States Coast Guard, where he has served on USCGC KIMBALL homeported in Honolulu, HI and USCGC MAUI homeported in Bahrain.

KAYLA HARRIS FONTAINE

HBCU All-Star
Kayla Harris Fontaine

When I left for VSU in 2012, I was on a mission to reinvent myself. I was eighteen years old, and I had been a "mama's girl" my entire life. But I knew that I could no longer be that timid, yet highly opinionated little girl, who hid behind her mom all the time. So, I decided to go away for school. I always knew that I wanted to attend an HBCU since I was old enough to understand what it meant to be black, which was probably since the age of fifteen. I was going through an identity crisis. Having a lighter complexion, I felt isolated. I never felt "black enough" to fit in. I thought that attending an HBCU would teach me how to fit in the black box and develop more friendships. Little did I know that it would teach me the exact opposite.

I found my home on the hill during Homecoming 2010, and it was love at first sight.

I instantly felt comfortable on campus. The entire vibe of the university felt like home. I knew that this was the place where I could grow, and ultimately, learn who I was.

I was so terrified when I left for school. I didn't know how I was going to do things on my own. I felt like I didn't know the first thing about being a college student. That's when I realized that mentors were so critical to my success, especially as an out-of-state student. One of the things you'll hear most often about HBCUs is that they offer a family-like environment.

VSU was no exception.

There were so many organizations that offered mentoring programs for freshmen; it was just a matter of finding one that was the right fit for me. In my search, I found my first organization, The Betterment of Brothers and Sisters, Inc. (BBS). The members were always active on campus and they shared a genuine love for our university. Everyone was so welcoming, and they held themselves to a higher standard, which appealed to me. I learned the basics from my big sisters and brothers in the organization.

Professionalism, service and a strong commitment to VSU are lessons that stick with me today. After I became an active member, I discovered that I could be a mentor to many.

One of the first pieces of advice I received when I got to State was, "Get involved!" I took it to heart—joining BBS and the honors program by the end of my freshman year. Through my organizations, I gave campus tours to prospective students, assisted with forums, and I signed up to mentor incoming freshmen. By the end of my sophomore year, I was recognized for my mentoring and selected to participate in the Thurgood Marshall College Fund (TMCF) Walmart First Generation Scholars mentorship program. This one experience changed the course of my career decisions forever.

After working hand in hand with TMCF staff, and taking into consideration my other talents, I knew I wanted to go into non-profit work. I felt like I could have more of an impact there than in radio.

I was lucky that VSU was always presenting a variety of opportunities to students. I presented my research on colorism and was able to share my personal experience with a large audience. Because of this, I was elected to the Virginia Collegiate Honors Council and served two terms as the only black female, HBCU representative on the board. I advocated for scholarship opportunities and for volunteer engagement, and I became highly respected by the students from other universities.

During the summer before my senior year, I received an email from a VSU staff member for an opportunity through The White House Initiative on HBCUs. It was for their HBCU all-star program. I had an opportunity to represent my university and become an advocate for the nation's HBCUs. Initially, I wasn't going to do it. I thought, *Am I ready for this large of an opportunity?* But inside, I knew I couldn't let this opportunity pass. My faculty mentor, Dr. Dan Roberts, who was director of the honors program at the time, encouraged me to go for the opportunity. He assisted with my application, and was committed to guiding me through my journey if I was selected. Before I walked on campus to start my senior year, I was notified that I had been chosen—out of over 400 applications—to be one of 83 HBCU all-star ambassadors. It was one of the proudest moments of my life.

As a part of the program, we were able to attend the national HBCU week-long conference that was held annually in D.C. Through this conference, we had sessions with celebrities, senators, HBCU presidents and advocates alike. I was surrounded by like-minded individuals from HBCUs across the country and I learned from so many perspectives. I can vividly remember one session we had with Benjamin Crump, Esq., the lawyer who represented Trayvon Martin's family. I sat with tears in my eyes as he recounted the events of his work with the Trayvon Martin case. He talked about civil responsibility and servant leadership, a term I had never heard before. It's a term that will guide the rest of my life.

By the end of my senior year, my resume was impressive. I had accomplished my dream of becoming a member of Delta Sigma Theta, Inc., and I graduated from Virginia State University on May 15, 2016 cum laude. I just knew that I was going to land my dream non-profit job and go on to live happily ever after, right? I had no idea that VSU had been preparing me for the ride of my life: the career world.

Upon graduation, I gained two jobs that I hated. This led to a period of unemployment and depression. I had all these amazing experiences in college, but I couldn't land a job in the real world. What had I done with all that VSU taught me? Did I really spend four years learning who I was, only to still not know where I wanted to be?

I forgot the main lesson I learned while at VSU: "You cannot fit into boxes that weren't designed for you. You have to step out of the box. Your potential is limited less." VSU taught me that the boxes that I tried to fit in didn't exist. I knew I would find where I was meant to be. Once I got there, I had all the tools to be successful.

Currently, I serve as a project manager for KABOOM!, which is the national non-profit dedicated to partnering with communities to end playspace inequity in areas of historic disinvestment for good. I work with external funders and communities across North America to build custom playspaces for the kids who need them most. In my position, I get to fly across the country, leading playspace projects of over 200 volunteers to build play infrastructure in just six hours. I also serve as a member of our Diversity, Equity and Inclusion Network, supporting our commitment to be a racially equitable organization. I also serve as a mentor to new project managers. Since coming to KABOOM! in 2018, I have built sixteen playspaces that serve hundreds of thousands of kids in over twelve states.

I recently had a review from a community I worked with in Flint, Michigan that said, "Kayla is the true definition of servant leadership." This sentiment shows the power of Virginia State University. Every opportunity that VSU gave me has led me to this point. Without Virginia State University, there is no impact. Without VSU, there is no me.

All that I am, and all that I accomplished, is because of my HBCU. Delegate Alfred W. Harris wanted a place, "...where all may get a drink from the fountain of knowledge." But it is so much more than that. HBCUs are incubators for the next generation of leaders. I am grateful that I can leave a little bit of that VSU love everywhere I go.

About Kayla Harris Fontaine

Kayla Harris Fontaine is an Experienced Project Manager with a demonstrated history of working with nonprofit organizations and Historically Black Colleges and Universities. With a Bachelor of Arts focused in Mass Communications from Virginia State University, Kayla leverages her skills to form strong relationships with stakeholders to influence changes in the lives of all children and young adults. In her current role as a Project Manager at KaBOOM! Kayla works directly with communities and other external stakeholders to engage their local communities through "Build it with KaBOOM!" playspace enhancement projects. During her tenure, she has successfully lead over 16 community build projects to bring new, safe playspaces for hundreds of kids across the United States. When she is not off building playgrounds, Kayla often works as a mentor and advocate for young adults in her community. Kayla is a Prince George's County, MD native and a proud member of Delta Sigma Theta Sorority, Inc.

Fallen Trojans

fam·i·ly

/ˈfam(ə)lē/

A group consisting of parents and children living together in a household.

All the descendants of a common ancestor.

A group of related things.

One thing that is unique about a Historically Black College and University is the extended family that you gain along the way. Many of us are eager to further our education as first-generation college students, while some use college as a getaway from their environment. We all come from various ethnicities, academic environments and living conditions. However, when you step foot on a HBCU, you embody that pride that comes with that university.

At Virginia State University, the moment you enter the Hill, you are a Trojan. Being a Trojan means something different to everyone, and that in itself is unique. Being a Trojan is what brings everyone together, in which bonds are created which are at times stronger than the blood bond that one may have with their own family. When a Trojan win, we all win. When a Trojan loses, we all lose. We are *one*. So, when we lose a Trojan, it cuts deeper than swords during ancient times.

Whether you shared every experience, a few, or none at all with a fallen Trojan, the loss still hits that same. It's a reminder of how short life really is and not to take the moments for granted. In this edition of The HBCU Experience: Virginia State University, we would like to pay our respects to a few of our fallen Trojans. We love and miss you all.

165

Tyler Alexander Wilson

March 10, 1993 to September 28, 2019

Curtis "Isaiah" Bunn

December 22, 1987 to February 10, 2020

Official Partners & Sponsors
of The HBCU Experience Movement, LLC

Baker & Baker Realty, LLC

Christopher Baker- CEO/Founder
Instagram: seedougieblake
Facebook: Christopher D. Baker
Email: baker.christopher@gmail.com

Bound By Conscious Concepts

Kathryn Lomax-CEO/Founder
Instagram: msklovibes223
Facebook: Klo-Kathryn Lomax
Contact: (972) 638-9823
Email: Klomax@bbconcepts.com

Dancer NC Dance District

Dr. Kellye Worth Hall
Instagram: divadoc5
Facebook: Kellye Worth Hall
Email: delta906@gmail.com

HBCU Wall Street

Torrence Reed & Jamerus Peyton-CEO/Founders
Facebook: HBCU Wall Street
Email: info@hbcuwallstreet.com

SPGBK

Springbreak Watches (SPGBK)

Kwame Molden- CEO/Founder
Instagram: SPGBK
Facebook: Kwame Molden
Email: info@springbreakwatches.com

Minority Cannabis Business Association

Shanita Penny- President
Instagram- Minority Cannabis
Facebook- MCBA.Org
Twitter- MinCannBusAssoc
LinkedIn- Minority Cannabis Business Association
Email-info@minoritycannabis.org
Website: www.MinorityCannabis.org
Phone: 202-681-2889

The Phoenix Professional Network

DJavon Alston-Owner/Founder
Instagram: thephoenixnetwork757
Facebook: DJavon Alston
Email: thephoenixnetwork757@gmail.com

Never2Fly2Pray

Jeffrey Lee Sawyer: Owner/Founder
Instagram: never2fly2pray
Facebook: Jeffrey Lee
Email htdogwtr@yahoo.com

Allen Financial Solutions

Jay Allen: Owner/Founder
Instagram: jay83allen
Facebook: Jay Allen
Email: allen.jonathan83@gmail.com

Holistic Practitioners

Tianna Bynum: CEO/Founder
Facebook: Tianna Bynum
Email tpb33@georgetown.edu

Journee Enterprises

Fred Whit: CEO/Founder
Facebook: Fred Whit
Instagram: frederickwjr
Email: frederickwjr@yahoo.com

Company: Ashley Little Enterprises, LLC

Ashley Little- CEO/Founder
Facebook: Ashley Little
Instagram: _ashleyalittle
Email: aalittle08@gmail.com

HBCU Pride Nation

CEO/ Founder: Travis Jackson
Instagram: hbcupridenation
Facebook: HBCU Pride Nation
Email: travispjackson@gmail.com

LK Productions

CEO/Founder: Larry King
Instagram: lk_rrproduction
Facebook: Larry King
Email: lk_production@yahoo.com

NXLEVEL TRAVEL (NXLTRVL)

Chief Executive Officer Hercules Conway
Chief Operating Officer Newton Dennis
Instagram-nxlevel
Instagram: herc3k
Facebook-Newton Dennis
Facebook: Hercules Conway
Email Address: info@nxleveltravel.com
Website: NXLEVELTRAVEL.COM

BLKWOMENHUSTLE

CEO/Founder: Lashawn Dreher
Instagram: blkwomenhustle
Facebook: Blk Women Hustle
Email: info@blkwomenhustle.com

PATTERSON, HARDEE & BALLENTINE, P.C.

Certified Public Accountants
Ashlee Brooks
Tax Associate
Email: ashleebrooks@hotmail.com

Campaign
Engineers

Campaign Engineers

Chris Smith, CEO/Founder
Instagram: csmithatl
Email Address: csmith1911@gmail.com

Boardroom Brand LLC

Samuel Brown III, CEO/Founder
Instagram:_gxxdy
Email Address: samuel.brown.three@gmail.com

HBCU 1010

Jahliel Thurman, CEO/Founder
www.hbcu101.com
Instagram: hbcu101
jahlielthurman@gmail.com

Uplift Clothing Apparel

Jermaine Simpson, CEO/Founder
UpliftClothingApparel.com
Instagram: Upliftclothingapparel

AC Events The Luxury Planning Experience

Amy Agbottah, CEO/Founder:
Email Address: amy@amycynthiaevents.com

PIXRUS Photo Booth logo

PIXRUS Photo Booth

Natan Mckenzie, CEO/Founder
Email Address: Natan.mckenzie@gmail.com
Instagram: pixrusghana

MMInvestments

Tarik McAllister, CEO/Founder:
Instagram: MMInvestments
Email Address: tarik@mmibuilders.com

AllThingsLoop

Kenya Nalls, CEO/Founder:
Email Address: staff@allthingsloop.com
Contact Number: 773-939-0680

Historically Black Since

CEO/Founder: Adrena Martin
Instagram: historicallyblacksince
www.hbcusince.com

February First

CEO/Founder: Cedric Livingston
www.februaryfirstmovie.com
Director/Writer February First: A Stride Towards Freedom

HBCU Times

David Staten, Ph.
hbcutimes@gmail.com
Facebook: HBCU Times
Instagram: hbcu_times8892
Bridget Hollis Staten, Ph.D

Swing Into Their Dreams Foundation

Pamela Parker and Lynn Demmons, Co-Founders
Email Address: swingintotheirdreams@gmail.com
Website: swingintotheirdreams.com

Harbor Institute

CEO/Founder: Rasheed Ali Cromwell, JD
Instagram: @theharborinstitute
Facebook: The Harbor Institute
Twitter: @harborinstitute
Email: racromwell@theharborinstitute.com

HBCU Pulse

CEO/Founder Randall Barnes
Website: hbcupulse.com
Instagram: @hbcupulse
Twitter: @thehbcupulse

SwagHer

Vice President Of Sales/Marketing Jarmel Roberson
Website www.swagher.net
instagram: swaghermagazine
Email Address: jroberson@swagher.net

H.E.R. Story Podcast

Janea Jamison|Creator
H.E.R. Story with J. Jamison
#Herstorymovement
IG : @herstory_podcast

HBCU Buzz

LUKE LAWAL JR.
lawal@lcompany.co
Fndr, CEO | (301) 221-1719 @lukelawal
L & COMPANY { *HBCU Buzz* | *Taper, Inc.* | *Root Care Health* }

Zoom Technologies, LLC

Torrence Reed - CEO/Founder
Instagram: torrencereed3
Email: support@zoom-technologies.co

KOE

Koereyelle Dubose CEO/Founder
Instagram: koereyelle
Email Address: hi@koereyelle.com

Yard Talk 101

Jahliel Thurman CEO/Founder
Instagram: YardTalk101
Website: YardTalk101.com

Chef Batts

Chef Batts

Keith Batts-CEO/Founder
Instagram: chefbatts
Email: booking@chefbatts.com

Johnson Capital

Marcus Johnson CEO/Founder
Instagram: marcusdiontej
Email: marcus@johnsoncap.com